**GOSPEL REFLECTIONS
FOR MINDS & HEARTS**

10 MINUTES MORE

*Other Books of Peter Malone
published by Coventry Press*

Hearts Burning Within Us
10 Minutes
Dear Movies
Christ Figures
Dear More Dear Movies

10 Minutes More is another delightful book from the pen of Fr Peter Malone MSC. It continues in the style the earlier book, *10 Minutes*.
These small books are created for short and focused reflections on Jesus.
The simple style belies a lifetime of scholarship and reflection on the Gospel accounts of Jesus; and Peter offers accessible insights into our favourite stories and connections to the great hero narratives of the Hebrew scriptures. Spirituality of the Heart weaves its way through the book drawing us to the Heart of God revealed in Jesus. Each chapter offers practical suggestions for reflection and ways in which we can embed the lessons from the stories into our everyday lives.
In our busy world, it is important to create moments to stop, to savour and to enjoy; and the invitation is for each of us to use this beautiful book for just that purpose.

ALISON MCKENZIE,
Secretary General of the Laity of the Chevalier Family

Peter Malone's recent book *10 Minutes, Gospel Reflections for Minds and Hearts* is a very valuable book for promoting discussion on many biblical events. The Team of Our Lady (Team 22 Vic east) of which I am the Spiritual Counsellor has used it as its study topic for many months at its regular gatherings. They have found it very interesting – an important quality in such a context – and informative. It has given the group an increased understanding of many biblical passages. It has provoked conversation and stimulated their interaction. It is written in a simple style, but to say it is simple does not mean it is not profound. Underlying it is a deep knowledge of scripture and a scholarship that, over the years, has enlarged the author's own insights into and understanding of the sacred texts.
Now he has written a new series of these Gospel reflections, *10 Minutes More*. I can strongly recommend it for both private reading and group discussion.

PAUL CASTLEY MSC,
author, *A Time for Hope* (Coventry Press)

GOSPEL REFLECTIONS
FOR MINDS & HEARTS

10 MINUTES MORE

PETER MALONE

COVENTRY PRESS

Published in Australia by
Coventry Press
33 Scoresby Road
Bayswater VIC 3153

ISBN 9781922589552

Copyright © Peter Malone MSC 2024

All rights reserved. Other than for the purposes and subject to the conditions prescribed under the *Copyright Act*, no part of this publication may be reproduced, stored in a retrieval system, or transmitted in any form or by any means, electronic, mechanical, photocopying, recording or otherwise, without the prior permission of the publisher.

Scripture quotations are from the *Jerusalem Bible* copyright © 1966 by Darton Longman & Todd Ltd and Doubleday and Company Ltd.

Catalogue-in-Publication entry is available from the National Library of Australia http://catalogue.nla.gov.au

Cover design by Ian James – www.jgd.com.au
Text design by Coventry Press
Set in EB Garamond

Printed in Australia

Contents

Foreword	ix
Jesus, the Story and the Storyteller	1
Why do Some Gospel stories of Jesus Appeal – and Others Not?	5
Mystical Experience – for Everyone?	8
Jesus in the Vein of Amos	11
Jesus in the Vein of Jeremiah – and not	14
Jesus in the Vein of the Suffering Servant	17
Jesus in the Vein of Ezekiel	20
Jesus in the Vein of Daniel	23
Jesus Transfigured. Moses and Elijah on the Mountain	26
Jesus not a Puritan. Cana	29
Jesus, Comforting the Afflicted	32
Jesus Shelterer	35
Jesus and the Grace of Endurance	38
No First Stone	41
Mary Magdalene, I Don't Know How to Love Him	44
Jesus Lifted up, Drawing us to Himself	48

Jesus, his Bequest, his new Commandment	51
Gethsemane Moments	54
Jesus, God's Final Word	57
Christ Reigns	60
Mary's Advent	63
Joseph, the Wise and Just Man	66
Profiling Peter's Faith Journey (Assisted by Carl Jung)	69
Thomas, According to the Gospel	72
Prepare Your Own Funeral Liturgy	75
Appendix: Gospel Pointers to the Heart of Jesus	80

Foreword

Readers of Peter Malone's initial *10 Minutes* will need no introduction to this sequel, *10 Minutes More*. It is essentially a book about Jesus, written in the same engaging, down-to-earth style, bringing the Gospel stories alive and closer to home.

Peter is a long-time scholar and teacher of the Sacred Scriptures. He has read the Bible many times, prayed it and taken it to heart. His writing is grounded in human experience, yet permeated by his awareness of God's ever-present love, witnessed and preached by Jesus. This is the spirituality of the heart, favoured by the Missionaries of the Sacred Heart, the religious congregation of which Peter has been a member for sixty years. I have known him and admired his extensive writing for all of those years.

Storytelling has a long tradition in humanity's desire to educate, inspire and support one another. In many cultures still, the stories are told by word of mouth, passing on the good word, at times personalising it, embellishing it. At the same time, the literary genre of storytelling is strong in religious writing. The Gospels belong in that tradition. Jesus himself was a storyteller – in this book, Jesus is both the story and the storyteller. Peter Malone then becomes a storyteller, making the Gospel stories readable and relevant to our times.

Peter brings his own wide experience to his reading and re-telling the stories. For example, he is as conversant with the books of the Old Testament as much as the New Testament, and often writes about the New in the light of the Old, evident in the initial reflections. As well, Peter uses his familiarity with movies – the cinematic genre of storytelling – to parallel examples of Jesus' life with our own experience and with contemporary issues in society: "divine action in lived human experience" (see "Jesus God's final word"). The reflection on the grace of endurance in this book is the perfect example of that.

This book is best read only one chapter at a time. Readers can dip into the book, reading slowly and thoughtfully. Reading a chapter will take only ten minutes of a busy day – though you can be sure to spend even more time reflecting on what you read. The stories are rich and deserve pondering and sharing with friends.

Brian Gallagher MSC
Author of *The Eyes of God* and *The Joy of Ageing*

Jesus, the Story and the Storyteller

For many decades, I have been fond of quoting an article by my late Redemptorist friend, Tony Kelly, writing about the incarnation. He reminded us that Jesus became story, from birth to death (or from conception to resurrection). His life is story.

To that extent, Jesus' life, as human, sharing our lives with us in every detail – joys, sorrows, the extremities of pain and suffering – becomes a parable of the human aspect of God's story. The Gospels narrate many stories of Jesus, enhancing his story with references and allusions to the Jewish Scriptures – think, say, of the Infancy narratives – often heightening the telling and impact of the story.

But Jesus is an arch-storyteller himself, a teller of parables, stories which interest, sometimes delight, sometimes shock, not just immersing us in the reality of the story details but, somehow or other, often subverting our expectations of what life is like or can be.

It might be helpful to consider Jesus' storytelling in each of the Gospels, highlighting his own experiences, his range of interests, his peeves, his complaints, his challenges as well as moments of delight and humour.

The Gospel of Mark is not a Gospel of parables. Rather, the shortest of the Gospels is an overview parable where Jesus himself is the story.

However, when we come to the Gospel of Matthew, we are told that the telling of parables is one of Jesus' preferred ways of teaching, like a scribe bringing out of his treasure house stories both old and new (13:52). Jesus had preached the coming of God's reign on earth, urging us all to repent to be ready for this wondrous presence of God. And so he explored the range of images of this reign of God – treasure in a field, a pearl of great price to be bought and valued, a wondrous catch of fish, weeds and wheat growing in a field, the sower scattering the seed on different types of soil, rich and meagre, the small mustard seed growing into the largest shrub. In this kind of storytelling, Jesus is a man of the land who knows crops, burning the weeds, harvesting. These parables are straightforward, no-frills.

At other times, there are moments of critical anger in his parables of fraudulent servants ensuring a post-sacking income, of servants who bully to get repayment. But there is also the theme of justice and bonus for labourers in the vineyard.

And, as with parables in Luke's Gospel, there are weddings to be filled with guests, there are administrators who are entrusted with finance to be worked on (but not buried).

As Matthew's Gospel comes to an end, prior to the passion and death of Jesus, the stories take on an apocalyptic tone, the wise and foolish bridesmaids and the invitation to the wedding and lack of alertness leading to exclusion. And the grand parable of the final judgment, the criterion for reward and punishment, the fullest love of neighbour whether sick, needy, in prison. This is the ultimate parable of God's reign on earth.

With the Gospel of Luke, we remember some of our favourite parables, reminded that Jesus really can tell a story (or that the Luke community wanted to ensure the memory that Jesus could tell a good story) – the Prodigal Son/Prodigal Father, Good Samaritan. And Jesus could tell a brief, effective parable – the boastful Pharisee praying to himself in comparison with the humble tax collector, the persistent and pestering widow hounding the unjust judge.

If Jesus showed us what God is like by what he said and did, he brings God into very human form in his parables. God is an extravagant father, extraordinarily permissive, allowing his son to make grievous mistakes, but on the lookout, ready to embrace him when he returns, celebrating his change of heart (as well as literally going out of the house to reach his humourless, law-abiding older son). God is the Good Samaritan, unlike the duty and ritual cleansing-obsessed priest and Levite passing by on the other side of the road, a rescuing God, a providing for hospitality God, with a message to the rather uppity lawyer: go and do the same yourself.

In the Gospel of John, Jesus again becomes the parable himself, the signs and wonders he performed, his living parable with water into wine at Cana, his conversation with the Samaritan woman at the well, feeding the thousands, the drama of the man born blind, Jesus raising his friend Lazarus from the dead... so that Jesus is Living Water, Bread of Life, Light of the World, Resurrection and the Life, and, in answer to doubting Thomas' question after the Last Supper, he is the Way, the Truth, the Life.

But, in John's Gospel, there is an explicit parable: the good shepherd. Jesus is certainly the good shepherd but, as shepherd, he is mirroring the care and shepherding of God. In fact, we might see this parable as a parable of the nature of leadership, true leadership. At the time of Jesus, there were plenty of bad shepherds, often rogues, small flocks, stealing from one another, desperate (but sufficiently redeemable to be invited to come to the manger at Bethlehem). The good shepherd not only cares but knows each sheep by name and, as we have seen in the other Gospels, Jesus' compassionate leadership surfaces when he sees the hassled crowd, like sheep without a shepherd. And in the parable, he is prepared to leave the 99 and the flock and go to seek the lost sheep – and rejoice when it is found.

The tradition of the church, of course, has referred to its leaders and shepherds but, sadly, so many during the centuries have proven rogues, bad shepherds. Pope Francis famously has urged leadership in the church to be that of good shepherds, going one more explicit step than Jesus, urging that they have the smell of the sheep.

So, yes, Jesus is the story and Jesus is The Storyteller.

Why do Some Gospel stories of Jesus Appeal – and Others Not?

Do you sometimes have a difficulty in looking at the Gospel Jesus, in listening to his words, in querying his actions when he seems to behave very differently from the way we might like him to behave?

Sometimes Jesus seems to have a short fuse, especially when asked questions by nit-picking scribes and Pharisees. And, it's more than a shock when he picks up the ropes and starts flailing in the temple, turning over the moneychangers' tables and ousting the buyers and sellers, even the animal sacrifices which were to be offered in the temple. He is kindly to little children, charming to their parents – and then suddenly denouncing those who harm children and more than suggesting millstones around their necks and their being cast into the depths of the sea.

I used to take comfort in what was told to us in scripture classes about the impact of each of the four Gospels, each in its different way, diverse perceptions and descriptions of Jesus. As explained to us, the tradition was that Mark's Gospel was very vivid, the eyewitness account of Mark, acting as secretary to Peter himself, a touch of accurate reportage. And we were told that the core of Mark's Gospel was incorporated into Matthew and

Luke. However, the tradition was that Matthew's Gospel was very emphatic in presenting Jesus' teaching, straight and plain, parables with no-frills. On the other hand, the word that was used over the centuries for Luke's Gospel was compassion. Luke's Gospel presented a very human Jesus, a nice Jesus (but, nevertheless, some of those short-fuse retorts). And we all realise that John's Gospel was very different, more symbolic, even mystical.

And this tradition was handed on for the best part of 2000 years.

Some years ago, I wrote a book called *The Same as Christ Jesus* (a reference to Philippians 2:5). The reason for writing it was that 20 or more years earlier, I had the good fortune to be introduced to a particular application of the personality theory of Swiss psychologist, Carl Jung. Two American women, mother and daughter, Katherine Briggs and Isabel Myers, worked in the early decades of the 20th century applying Jung's ideas, finding practical ways of indicating how we might appreciate these personality traits in ourselves. Being practical Americans, they devised questionnaires, The Myers-Briggs Type Indicator (MBTI). It was emphasised that this was not a psychological test. The observations were neither good or bad, right or wrong – but, over to those interested, *indications*.

I had the good fortune of meeting Sister Margaret Dwyer, a Sister of Charity from Melbourne who brought Type to Australia in the early 1980s, to the Catholic Education Office. It was she who pointed out the relationship between Jung's ideas and that old Gospel tradition about the perspectives of each Gospel. She noted that Mark's Gospel was very strong in what we might call Sense detail (more than in Matthew or Luke). In looking at Matthew's Gospel and the emphasis on teaching, the presentation of Jesus is very strong, principled, logical, Thinking criteria for decisions. While Jesus does teach in Luke's Gospel, there are many more humane stories, parables, personal encounters, Jesus making decisions on more personal criteria (and running the risk, by association with open sinners, of condemnation by the religious authorities). Feeling criteria for decisions. Jung's fourth function was the opposite of the Sensing, the delight in the hunches and possibilities, Intuition. And, with only John's Gospel and its mystical tones left, no difficulty in seeing this Gospel as Intuitive.

This perception of the different Gospels and the way they portray Jesus reflects the variety of personalities there were in those initial gospel communities, the three years of travelling with Jesus, the decades of sharing of memories before they were written down, then the process of collating the stories, the interpretations of the stories, actually writing them.

The purpose of this reflection is to highlight how each of us has our own personal preferences, the way we are, the way we act, the way we perceive people and situations. Which means, of course, that we will identify more particularly with specific Gospel episodes and not be attracted or enticed by others. But, as Jung suggested, we have to grow, to incorporate the unfamiliar traits with those with which we are comfortable. I might be more at home with Luke's Gospel but there is the continual challenge to the clarity, objectivity, challenges and demands of the teaching in Matthew's Gospel.

It's time to end this particular reflection. It was intended to open up ideas and possibilities – and, if this catches your attention, there are quite a number of books and articles on the MBTI and spirituality. And, if you would find it helpful, and if you could find a copy, I elaborated a lot of these ideas in *The Same as Christ Jesus*.

Mystical Experience
– for Everyone?

Do you have experiences which could be called "mystical"? Or, are these experiences, mystical experiences, limited to the prayer of Jesus himself, in union with the father, to the classic Mystics in the deserts of the early Christian centuries, or the Middle Ages, or 16 century Spain with Teresa of Avila and John of the Cross? Back in the day, that seemed to be what we thought. Mysticism was beyond most of us.

The question arose in a discussion about mystics and saints, wondering whether there was a difference. The conversation continued about recognising some heroic people during their lives, their service of others, self-sacrifice, their faith and prayer, saints. But, of course, saints with the S have to be recognised by the church, long processes, investigations, miracles through their intercession... And that seems to cut out most of us!

But, mystics. Interestingly, some of the mystics have not been canonised, perhaps most notably Julian of Norwich with her reassurance that "all will be will".

But us!

Remember Jesus' words, his injunction against babbling, repetitious and ostentatious praying in public, but rather going into our rooms quietly and communing with God, his gift of "The Lord's Prayer", and the various scenes of his own praying, retreating for the night in silent prayer, his agony in Gethsemane, his prayer on the cross.

In our conversation about mystics in everyday life we wondered what these everyday mystical experiences would be like. And then there were memories of Anglo-Catholic author, Evelyn Underhill, who wrote as early as 1911 on mysticism, and published in 1914, *Practical Mysticism* – and she died in 1941. Which led to the reminder that eminent theologian, Karl Rahner, had written on *The Mystical Way in Everyday Life*. Strong credentials.

We have been blessed that in recent times that there have been many movements, inside the Church, within Christianity, beyond Christianity, where many people of different cultures want to pause, centre (centring prayer), contemplate with mantras, experience mindfulness.

Looking back, Novice Masters in those days had a special urging for us, small prayers that we could remember and pray as the thought came to us, no matter where. The word was "Aspirations", those little prayers that took only a brief moment. Were they our moments of mystical prayer without our realising it?

But then, a daring suggestion was made. Could an atheist have mystical experiences? Why not?

Which led us to talk about "transcending" our ordinary experiences, in going beyond the ordinary, a different consciousness and awareness, possible for someone who did not believe in any God to transcend their limited experiences, an awareness of the deeper inner self and its potential, and amazed awareness at the wonder of the universe, cosmic mysticism, so to speak.

And if that is possible for the atheist, what about the believer? Further transcending of our day-to-day experiences of God, graced experiences, wonder? And, the cautious reminder that this experience of wonder and transcendence can be in the midst of sadness and suffering, not only in joy and happiness.

A story and an insight which has sustained me since the 1960s. One of the Jesuit lecturers at the Gregorian University, Father Karel Truhlar, from Yugoslavia, offered a special short course called Theology of Recreation. Just a thing to make a connection between cinema and theology. One of his important references was to another Jesuit, Joseph Marechal, from the University of Louvain. Marechal's insight was this: with every finite experience, there is always an openness to more, always more, and, as he said, an openness to the infinite. Which believers name, of course, as God.

Which means that every finite experience, every small experience, has the potential to open us to the transcendent, to God. Not that we are always conscious of this. But, in those moments, in those experiences, which take us in some ways outside ourselves, beyond ourselves, believer and nonbeliever like, there is the mystical.

Which, reassuringly (but not to dampen any of our sainthood ambitions and hopes) means that we can be mystics even if not saints.

Jesus in the Vein of Amos

We remember that the prophet Micah (6:8) exhorts us to "act justly" – and he is channelling the prophet, Amos. But what about Amos himself, something in the tradition of his predecessors, Elijah Elisha, not so much the acting justly but exhorting all those who heard them to have a justice consciousness?

In Jesus' time, some thought he was Elijah come again. And, in so many ways, he was a new embodiment of those older Hebrew prophets. Perhaps we could say that he was Amos come again.

The main impact of Amos was his prophetic capacity, in God's name, for denunciation of injustice. Can there be a spirituality of denunciation? Is that how we can interpret Amos and Jesus? One of the problems that immediately arises is the language and tone of denunciation. There is a fair amount of what we might call invective. There is a lot of rhetorical invective. Amos didn't mince words. And, we realise, that often, in fact very often, Jesus didn't mince words either.

There is a key passage in Amos 7 where the prophet is challenged by the religious leaders, asking what business he has to come into the city of Bethel and disturb the peace. Amos doesn't quietly explain himself, justify himself – rather, his response is a retort. The religious authorities have referred to him as a seer (with a sneer). But he is confident in himself, confident that God has called him (when God speaks who can but prophesy?), proclaim his authenticity, nor is he just one of the local professional prophets. He speaks with the authority of God. He reminds them of the covenant agreements, that the people remain faithful to God's justice (which they have not), that God is always faithful and had promised to reach out to them whenever they turn away. Prophets would be sent to challenge them, for forgiveness, for a new spirit of justice.

Like Amos, Jesus had to explain himself when the religious authorities wanted him to justify himself. They attacked him for casting out devils in the devil's name. Like Amos, he retorted, challenging them on their own practices. In those retorts, Jesus would turn the tables on the religious leaders (and, when provoked, we know that he could literally overturn tables as well).

So, a question for the spirituality of denunciation is: what is the place of anger, what is the place of rage? How do you express the anger rightly and righteously? What is the language and feeling of appropriate rage?

Amos identified with those who were poor, impoverished, victims of the wealthy and their lavish lifestyles (he warned: "the sprawler's revelry is over!", 6:7). And this is what Jesus did, even more explicitly in his having compassion on the people who were like sheep without a shepherd, sharing their rough life with them (foxes have holes...), going to meals with prostitutes and fraudulent money collectors.

But, every so often, in the book of Amos, there are small lyrical passages, praise and wonder, God creator. Which gave Amos more than a touch of authenticity in his denunciations. Jesus did the same, "I bless you father, Lord of heaven and earth...", a touch of authenticity and authority to his preaching.

One of the best examples of Jesus denouncing selfish behaviour, especially of the priestly and Levite castes, the religious authorities, is his parable of the Good Samaritan. The seemingly rather stuffy lawyer who had asked Jesus about the law and was told this parable in return. In the vein of those who continually tried to discredit Jesus, he had asked Jesus the key question, "And who is my neighbour?". Jesus' confronting question is the asking of who fulfilled love of neighbour, and who, despite appearances and opinions, was the true neighbour: the Samaritan. It seems the lawyer could not bring himself to say out loud the word, Samaritan. And what does Jesus say – not congratulations, hundred percent correct? But in quiet Amos' tones, a spirituality of denunciation and challenge, "go and do the same yourself".

Jesus in the Vein of Jeremiah – and not

Actually, the young Jeremiah does not present much of a foreshadowing of Jesus at all. In chapter 1, we hear that he is young, diffident, reluctant, arguing that he does not know how to speak and that he is a child. This is not the pattern of God's prophet. But, although Jeremiah was graced, even in the womb, God is not very happy with him. It is as if God took a handful of his words and jammed them into Jeremiah's face, pressed them on his lips, and told him, there, go out and preach my word whether you and my word are well-received, accepted, or not.

Which, of course, is what poor Jeremiah did, with some terrible repercussions for his self-consciousness as a prophet, for his being mocked, for his being physically assaulted, tossed down a well. He is the prophet of Lamentations and, strangely, he finally disappears from sight, almost anonymously, leaving the stricken Jerusalem and being taken down to Egypt.

Not exactly an introduction to Jesus in the vein of Jeremiah.

But, of course, there are two very important resemblances: first, Jeremiah's communicating the news of God's love and affection and his transforming hearts from stone to human. This is all in chapter 3 and 31, the opening with God speaking of an everlasting love and constant affection for us. Later, the promise that God would excise our hearts of stone, would implant in us human hearts, full of love, on which the Ten Commandments, no longer in stone, will be written in our human hearts which then become the new arks of the covenant, the embodiment of God's covenant pledges. Not necessary for us to teach God's love because it is written in all of our hearts.

Jesus and his love in word and action is definitely in this Jeremiah vein.

And the second resemblance to Jeremiah can be summed up in Jeremiah's anguished trust: I commit my cause to you (11:20; 20:10) and echoed by the Servant in the book of Isaiah (48). In fact, Jesus transcends Jeremiah's commitment, not following the prophet's lead in calling down vengeance on all his enemies, but submitting "like a lamb to the slaughter" to whatever God asks of him.

Jesus, in his whole life and passion can be seen to be saying to the Father, I commit my cause to you.

It is there, at the beginning of his ministry, Jesus tempted and tested by the Satan, banishing him and setting his eyes clearly on his mission, the first commitment to God's cause. This is reinforced soon after by his proclamation that the reign of God is at hand and that he is preaching repentance and an invitation to all to commit their cause to God.

And Jesus makes space at important times during his ministry, renewing his commitment, retreating to silence and prayer, relying on the Father as he comes down from the mountain and chooses the Twelve, as he flees the crowd who want to making king, wanting him to be leader for the wrong cause.

This commitment of his cause to God is manifest in the garden of Gethsemane, Jesus in anguish, experiences of self-doubt, "is it me?" (The repeated striking question in Dennis Potter's play, *Son of Man*). Mark's Gospel says that Jesus sweated blood. Alone, his disciples sleeping, fully realising the extremes that were being asked of him in terms of physical suffering and death, he does ask that this ordeal might be taken away – but, a re-phrasing of I commit my cause to you, "not my will, but yours be done".

During his passion, Jesus stands up for himself, asserting himself and his commitment, first to Annas when he is spat on and insulted, then to Caiaphas, his surprising (shocking!) claim that he is the fulfilment of Daniel's prophecy of the Son of Man leading the chosen into the presence of God - and Jesus is rebuked and condemned for being blasphemous.

Scourged, crowned with thorns, mock purple cloak, he is brought into the presence of Pontius Pilate who proclaims, "Here is the man", Jesus having proclaimed his kingship, not of this world, and now condemned to carry across and be crucified on Calvary.

In the worst of human situations, in ignominious crucifixion as a criminal, humiliated, sharing the extremes of our human experiences in suffering, Jesus bows his head, breathes forth his spirit, "it is accomplished".

In this ultimate commitment, breathing forth this Spirit, embraced in death by the Father, Jesus becomes the risen Lord.

Jesus in the Vein of the Suffering Servant

Jesus is the Servant

The four Servant Songs, found in the second section of Isaiah, Deutero-Isaiah, made a mark in the consciousness of Israel, especially during the woes of the exile in Babylon following the destruction of Jerusalem and of the temple and the disappearance of the Ark of the Covenant. They continued to make their mark in the consciousness of the early Christian communities, in the writing of the Gospels, in the Second Letter of Peter, Pauline allusions, in interpreting the life, suffering and death of Jesus in the light of the pattern of the prophetic Suffering Servant.

In Holy Week, we have the occasion of hearing the Songs in the first reading of the Eucharist, culminating in the fourth Song during the Good Friday Liturgy. We can take the opportunity of noting some of the key elements in the Servant Songs which made such a strong impact – and still do.

For reference, here are the key passages of the Songs –

- Isaiah 42:1–4;

- Isaiah 49:1–6;

- Isaiah 50:4–11;

- Isaiah 52:13–53:12.

The Servant is not a servant in the menial sense. Rather, the Servant is a prophet, someone who listens attentively to God's word, living it, communicating it. And, so, in the first Song, God "delights" in the Servant, the Servant in whom God is well pleased. And we remember that at Jesus' baptism, at the Transfiguration, God's voice is heard, Jesus the beloved, in whom the Father is well pleased. And, with our Trinitarian perspective, we realise that the pleasing Servant is given the gift of the Spirit, in the Song as well as at the baptism.

This gift of the Spirit is also a call to the service of the Servant: to bring justice to the nations, a vision beyond the chosen people of Israel to the wider world. And, after his baptism, Jesus begins his ministry of true justice but, acknowledging that if God's reign is to prevail, we all need to look at ourselves, to repent.

The other aspect of the first Servant Song is the quality of the Servant's mission: not a bombarding mission, rather ease in mission, gentle, no crying out, no shouting in the streets. Not that the Servant is not forthright. And Jesus, at times, is very forthright. But neither of them put out the smouldering wick, or crush the bruised reed. Conversion usually takes time.

In the second Song, the Servant is identified as a Chosen one. Like his predecessor, Jeremiah, he has been chosen and consecrated in the womb, to be a prophet to the nations, his words both healing and challenging, and, as we remember that the letter to the Hebrews says that the word of God is likened to two-edge sword, piercing consciousness. And so, Luke has his annunciation to Mary story, Matthew has Joseph's bewilderment at Mary's condition but shielding her, and the prophecies that the child's name is Jesus, saviour.

But the second Song also reminds us that the prophetic mission is not easy, not smooth, not always well received – and, the Servant, echoing the frequent phrase of Jeremiah, declares "I commit my cause to you".

And this optimism pervades the opening of the third Song, the Servant eagerly waking in the morning, attentive, with a listening ear like a disciple, an enthusiastic tongue to speak God's word. And then the mood changes. We know the phrases that are used to torment the Servant because John's Gospel uses them when Jesus stands before the high priest, Annas. His enemies strike him. They pull out his beard. They spit. We can expect worse to come – and it does. But, there is a contrast between the third Song with its urge to vengeance against persecutors with Jesus on the cross forgiving his enemies, for they do not know what they do.

But, it is the fourth Song that had the greatest influence in the early Christian communities and with us all. The Song opens with some moments of hope, the Servant prospering and respected, but it soon moves into the sorrow and suffering description of the "man of sorrows, acquainted with grief", vivid descriptions of the man despised, rejected. And people turn away from looking at him. And the powerful reaction word, appalled. Something of a blueprint for the description of Jesus' passion and death.

But, it is the motivation that expresses the height of self-giving, self-sacrifice, the servant bearing his humiliation, his pain, stricken, struck by God, pierced, crushed, for the sake of others – and the slaughter-imagery, the lamb, but by his wounds we are healed.

"... surrendering himself to death, and letting himself be taken for a sinner, while he was bearing the faults of many and praying all the time for sinners."

Then there is a certain calmness, a quiet grave, the gift of a rich man. But, even though at the time of the Servant, there was no appreciation of a life after death, yet there is some hope of vindication, even of Resurrection.

So, it is not Jesus in the vein of the Suffering Servant – Jesus is the fulfilment, he is the Suffering Servant.

Jesus in the Vein of Ezekiel

Do we often think of the connections between Jesus and the prophet, Ezekiel? Here are some moments to do so. He lived more than 500 years before the coming of Jesus.

When we look at the first chapter of the rather long book of Ezekiel's prophecies, he emerges as something of a strange character, an imaginative visionary, trying to describe in visuals and in motion, something of the glory of God. (And the influence with four heads, human, lion, ox, eagle, images associated with each of the Gospels.) And then he eats part of the parchment with God's word – and "it tasted as sweet as honey". While there are many oracles and prophecies throughout the book, Ezekiel is also noted for a number of symbolic prophetic actions. It was one of the ways of communicating in disastrous times, the invasion of the Babylonians, the destruction of the temple, the disappearance of the Ark of the Covenant, the dispersion of the people, exile. And he saw the glory of God rising out of the temple, going into exile with the people. But he lived to see the glory of God rise from Babylon and return to Jerusalem.

Ezekiel lived in difficult times. So did Jesus. And the Gospel writers sometimes seem to see Jesus as the Ezekiel of his times. Time of transition, time of Roman occupation, and, after Jesus'death, the destruction of the Temple and the new phase of the Jewish diaspora.

Ezekiel communicated by performing symbolic actions, like showing the people their future by dressing as a beggar, miming leaving through the city walls, indicating exile, so the Gospels are full of Jesus and his symbolic actions. Consider the way the stories of Jesus' miracles are told. Often with some drama, weeping with the widow of Naim, summoning Lazarus out of the tomb, the drama of the raising of the daughter of Jairus. But, to appreciate the Last Supper, we can see Jesus as powerfully symbolic, holding up the bread and declaring "this my body", holding up the wine, "this my blood".

But, the important connections are how Jesus takes up the themes of Ezekiel.

The glory of God has been noted already, and, in John's Gospel, declaring that in miracles Jesus let his glory be seen. Ultimately, Jesus speaks of being lifted up, a time of glory when the hour comes.

Probably the best-known comparison is that of Ezekiel's shepherd chapter, chapter 34, and the frequent Gospel references to sheep, the good shepherd, lost sheep, separation of the good sheep... Since David was a shepherd, shepherd imagery was associated with the kings, and, when the kings were unfaithful and disappeared, shepherd qualities were attributed to the best leader. Jesus, son of David, not just the good shepherd, but the best shepherd.

One of the best, hopeful passage in Ezekiel is found in chapter 36, paralleling Jeremiah 31 and the new heart that God gives the people, the pledge of covenant fidelity, but also introducing the themes of water, cleansing, refreshing, this water poured over the people, God's baptism of the people, and an affirmation that this God will be their God, they will be God's people. Later, when the glory cloud returns to Jerusalem, Ezekiel has a vision of the new temple, and water flowing from its side, a trickle, gathering force, a torrent, an image that receives new life in John's Gospel, Jesus speaking of the destruction of the Temple but its being raised up in his body, and the image of blood and water flowing from the side of Jesus on the cross.

And, not to forget chapter 37, premonitions of resurrection, the dead bones in the valley, the breath of God, their rattling together, coming to life. It took some centuries before these resurrection, life after death themes, took hold in the minds and imaginations of the people. Later in Ezekiel's prophecies, the tone becomes more apocalyptic, vast imaginative battles, Gog and Magog, which also influences the way the Gospels had Jesus speak of disastrous times, symbolic images which led into the final writings of the New Testament, the apocalyptic book of Revelation.

We realise that Jesus is in the vein of Ezekiel, perhaps, more often than we might have thought.

Jesus in the Vein of Daniel

While we find the book of Daniel situated amongst the oracles of the prophets, Daniel was not one of the classical prophets. Rather, the book of Daniel seems more like a historical novel with an aim of morale boosting. It comes from the second century before Jesus, the time of invasion, oppression, persecution by Antiochus of Syria, the resistance of the Maccabees. It can be seen something in the vein of the books of Judith, Esther, Tobit, entertaining narratives, strong central characters, the defence of God's people against tyrants...

But, the authors of the book of Daniel decided to set it in past times, the earlier sixth century BC invasion of the kingdom of Judah, the destruction of the temple, loss of the Ark of the Covenant, the people going into exile. Daniel is in exile with the people, in Babylon, confronting the invading king, Nebuchadnezzar, and a confrontation with his son, Belshazzar, the episode of the vision of the writing on the wall and the king's doom.

Before I focus on the two significant narratives from the book, I thought I would do a Google exercise, search for the connection between Daniel and Jesus. I was rather taken aback to find on some Protestant websites, a large number of connections between the two, parallels between the two. I was not sure I was convinced – perhaps because I had my own agenda which I would now like to explore.

However, what I wanted to do in this reflection was to focus on two major themes from the book itself. But, I did also want to mention the presence of angels in the book of Daniel, Michael, the warrior, who would appear in the book of Revelation, and Gabriel, God's messenger who would announce the fullness of time (nine, 12), the messenger that Luke's gospel chose to come to Mary in Nazareth and announce the coming of the son of David.

There was always some dispute about whether Daniel, chapter 13, should be part of the Scriptures, rejected by the Reformers and others as apocryphal. But it is a very good story, the focus on Susanna, a woman of integrity, the perversions of the religious leaders, leering, stalking, threatening. The targeting of an innocent woman. And it is the young Daniel who comes to her defence, questioning the two elders, catching them out in contradictory evidence, vindicating Susanna.

Commentators on John's story of the woman taken in adultery, her being denounced by the religious elders, Jesus defending her, sets up Jesus as the new Daniel. However, there is a greater depth to the story in John, the woman is not innocent, she is guilty. The elders are correct in their accusations – but merciless in their demands that she be punished, death by stoning. Jesus is the new Daniel, challenges their mercilessness, offers whoever is innocent the opportunity to cast a first stone, but they skulk away. And Jesus, saving the woman, saving the guilty woman, sending her to her future life, repentant, might say "a greater than Daniel is here".

The other connection between Jesus and the book of Daniel is the vision in chapter 7, God described as "the Ancient of Days", holding court, the presence of the mass of those who are saved, and the leader of the saved, appearing and coming into the presence of God, one "like the Son of Man", a figure of power, glory – and salvation. One might say it is the last powerful vision, this time prophetic, in the Old Testament Scriptures.

And its importance for Jesus. We remember that during his trials before Annas and Caiaphas, Caiphas becomes more desperate that Jesus condemn himself. He demands that Jesus tell the court who he is – and Jesus answers with the quotation from Daniel. Jesus is the Son of Man, the saviour, about to suffer and die, but who will rise and lead the faithful into God's presence.

Jesus spoke his death warrant, quoting Daniel, Caiaphas declaring that Jesus has blasphemed and must die. We remember this text. We hear it in Lent in Holy Week and the narratives of the passion, but, it would be valuable to go back to Daniel 7 and remember the richness of this vision, what it meant to Jesus, and the hope that it offers us in our fidelity and commitment.

Jesus Transfigured. Moses and Elijah on the Mountain

For many of us, Jesus' transfiguration is a favourite story. We find versions in Matthew, Mark and Luke. It is told again, in the voice of Peter in 2 Peter And, the liturgy provides us with the opportunity each year to hear the story, the second Sunday of Lent and on the Feast, August 6th. On the first Sunday of Lent, the church invites us to focus on the very human Jesus, at the beginning of his ministry, out in the desert for those symbolic 40 days, hungry, the Satan, the biblical adversary, testing and tempting. We can identify with the Jesus tested and tempted, we can hope that we will always be effective in our rebuttal as Jesus was.

But, on the second Sunday of Lent, our focus is on Jesus letting his glory be seen. We are invited to focus on the Jesus who is to experience his passion and death but who will triumph, a glory in risen life.

And it all takes place on a mountain. Popular devotion – and tourism – has focused on Mount Tabor in Galilee and pilgrims continue to visit the "site" of the Transfiguration. Perhaps you heard in the 70s that the Israeli government was asked to consider a cable car extending from the top of Mount Tabor to Nazareth.

What would Jesus, Mary and Joseph say! However, the plans were not followed through.

But, the mountain is important. As it was in the history of the Hebrew people. Mount Sinai was the mountain par excellence. And, we are invited in our contemplation of the Transfiguration to keep Mount Sinai in our consciousness. After all, the mountain has the symbolism of being where earth meets heaven, where God can come to earth, so to speak, an encounter with us. And, as we re-read Exodus 19, it was where the Hebrew people in their escape from Egypt, liberated from the Egyptians, in the person of Moses, encountered the God who is. Sinai is the mountain of the old covenant.

It was there, in the saga tradition of the Pentateuch, that God pledged, freely, to be faithful always, loving-kind and just to the people, no matter what. Unconditional covenant. And, through the darkness, God's glory appeared, shining through, even transforming the face of Moses so that he had to cover it. Now, on Mount Tabor, there is Jesus, the new covenant himself, good freely given, God's pledge incarnate.

And, it was at Mount Sinai that Moses received the Ten Commandments, the law of the covenant. And, here on Mount Tabor is Jesus, who will urge the New Covenant Law, to love one another as he has loved us.

It is no wonder that Moses is there. He is highlighting how Jesus is the new Moses.

And, with Elijah being there, it means that the Transfiguration is placed in the context of the law and the prophets. Elijah, despite (or because of) some of the fierceness of his symbolic actions, is the first of the prophets. The prophets, of course, were the mouthpieces of God, by what they said, and by their actions and lives. And it Elijah who is the reminder that Jesus is God's very prophetic word incarnate, in everything he said and did. It is no wonder that Elijah is there, highlighting how Jesus is a new Elijah, the new prophet. And, in each version, this is confirmed by the voice of God proclaiming that Jesus is the beloved/chosen son, that we should listen to him.

This is the declaration of God at Jesus' baptism, and, these are the words that come from the first Servant Song (Isaiah 42), the Songs highlighting the ministry of the servant, gentle mission, proclaiming salvation, but not listened to, persecuted, becoming the servant-lamb of God, giving up life for others, raised to the fullness of life by God. This was important in the early church, the memory of the words of the Father heard on the holy mountain, when they saw his glory (2 Peter 1: 16-18).

Lukes's Gospel mentions that Jesus was speaking with Moses and Elijah about his passion – greater risen glory after suffering and death?

That is the focus on Jesus. What about the focus on Peter, James and John? And should we identify with them? They had been especially called, privileged, invited to share this special experience, invited to witness Jesus and his life-giving to the daughter of Jairus. They were witnesses to Jesus as the word of God, as fulfilling the law of love.

But, while it was sleepy on Mount Tabor, and they were overwhelmed yet alert, Peter even wanting to stay there, our minds go forward to Gethsemane, Jesus' agony in the garden, their being invited to share at this beginning of his passion, their failure, their sleep. Each second Sunday of Lent, while we are amazed at the Transfiguration experience, we are also dismayed at the ultimate experience of Peter, James and John – here is a discipleship and fidelity challenge at the beginning of Lent.

While each Gospel says that this experience refers to Jesus rising from the dead but that, for the time being, that was to be their secret. But, after being overwhelmed, they look up, as we must, and see only Jesus.

Jesus not a Puritan. Cana

It was a temptation to use the word "wowser" instead of "Puritan" in this title. However, I wonder how far outside Australian shores is the word 'wowser' used let alone recognised. Puritan will have to do! (And remembering that Puritans are concerned that someone, somewhere, is enjoying him or herself!)

It is interesting to realise that the Cana story must have remained popular in its re-telling during the early decades of the church's life and development, finding its form in John's Gospel at the end of the first century. While it is significant, as we know, as the first of the signs and wonders that Jesus performed and his disciples believed in him, it is also an opportunity to know something about the character and personality of Jesus himself. We are reading between the lines because the lines themselves are focused on the sign and its meaning.

Cana is near enough to Nazareth. Mary was invited to this wedding feast. Jesus, already in his ministry, was popular enough to be invited, along with the disciples. Jesus had absorbed the Hebrew scriptural tradition in praise of marriage, of the delight in spouses celebrating their love, lyrical romantic passages on love from *The Song of Songs*, and, all the time, the image of God's love being like that of the spouses, especially written of in the love of the bridegroom for the bride. The Scriptures praise the sexual love of marriage, sexual in the fullest sense. So, Jesus, though a celibate himself, happy to go to a wedding – and he later told parables about feasts, the need to fill up with the hall with guests, and bridesmaids who were wise and others who were not.

And a wedding feast. Again, the Hebrew scriptural tradition frequently enjoys meals, feasts and celebrations, hospitality. In fact, as the centuries continued, the feast becomes an image of the heavenly feast in which we will all celebrate, and an emphasis on good food but, again frequently in the Scriptures, the praise of wine, 'fine strained wines', and wine that gives joy to the human heart. Jesus was comfortable at meals, hospitality, celebrations – even criticised in comparison with his austere cousin, John, for being something of a glutton and wine-bibber. In his own time, Jesus certainly did not have the reputation of being a Puritan.

The story seems to suggest the Jesus was sociable, friendly, good company, able to enter into the spirit of the feast (and some of the Jesus' films shows Jesus joyfully dancing). The telling of the story also implies that Jesus was a dutiful son, strongly influenced by his mother even as he questioned whether he should be letting his power be seen. And, when the vessels were all filled with water, no cheap miracle, only the best wine!

But, of course, that is not the major point of the Johannine Community wanting to tell the story. The Gospel was going to culminate in the fulfilment of Jesus mission, his suffering and death, his ultimately breathing forth his spirit in complete self-sacrifice, symbolised by the blood and water flowing from his pierced side, leading to the Father accepting the complete life-giving, Jesus ultimate 'yes', and raising him to new risen life. Jesus resurrected. Jesus' glory. This was Jesus' 'Hour'. John's Gospel appreciates that the changing of the water into wine was in anticipation of Jesus' final manifestation in glory.

His disciples were led to believe in him after this first sign, given in Cana, but it was often a struggling journey, comprehending other signs, when Jesus said he was Living Water, Bread of Life, Light of the world, Good Shepherd and, ultimately, the Way, the Truth, the Life.

So, in the context of the wedding celebration and the potential disaster with the lack of wine, in ordinary circumstances, appreciating the personality of Jesus as he was, the disciples began to take further steps in their life journey of faith in him.

Jesus, Comforting the Afflicted

I don't think I use the word 'afflicted' very often, if at all and wondering whether you do. It is there in translations of the Psalms, 'When I said I am sorely afflicted' (115;1). And, in the Litany of Loretto, Mary is called, Comforter of the Afflicted. (At the foot of the cross, Mary is afflicted by the hatred towards Jesus, but channels into comforting her son,) But, afflicted is a word that nags at the consciousness. It is a sad word, a grieving word, 'comfortless'.

See my affliction and save me. (Psalm 118 (119), 153)

It seemed best to do a little Googling, checking on the meaning of 'afflicted'. I responded positively to the suggested meaning: the state of being in pain. That is certainly a state that needs comforting, as much relief as possible, compassionate support when relief does not seem possible.

But, there was a caution. The suggestion was that the word not be used to describe a disability. This is a case of sensitivity towards those who experience their disability, who live with it, make good with it.

So, Jesus comforted those who were in states of pain, offering sympathy, empathy in the way that his comfort is offered and given.

You will have your own favourite stories. These are some of mine.

Jesus, Comforting the Afflicted

Somehow or other, it is the healing of the leper in Mark 1:31. That is a favourite. There is an immediate rapport between Jesus and the leper, the leper who risked breaking the law by coming close to Jesus out of the humiliating quarantine exile where he could not even utter his name but had to cry out "unclean". The leper makes his appeal to Jesus, "... If you want to...". And the immediate response Jesus experiencing a man in a state of pain, "Of course, I want to". And, not just a sentiment. Jesus reaches out and touches the man with leprous sores, risking infection and law-breaking, offering healing.

And what of Jesus expressing his emotion? With tears? The physical outpouring of inner empathy, his feelings enabling him to enter within those feelings of the afflicted person, the person in the state of pain, especially grief. In the encounter with the widow of Naim, Luke 7, he wept. And, sharing the grief of his close friends, Martha and Mary, the Gospel verse is: Jesus wept. And in his sharing the grief, Jesus himself needs comfort.

It was not exactly the same when he raised the daughter of Jairus to life. He knew what Jairus and his wife were suffering with the death of their little daughter. But it is Mark's version which has that empathetic Jesus' touch, "give her something to eat". And, speaking of something to eat, we might remember Peter and the pain of his ill mother-in-law, she recovers – and Jesus and the disciples being rewarded by the grateful mother-in-law sitting them down for one of her meals.

Another favourite, in the rather full of version in Mark's Gospel, is the episode on the way to the house of Jairus. This is the story of the elderly woman who had suffered from a haemorrhage for so many years, quietly and unobtrusively in pain, but with a confidence that if she could just touch the hem of Jesus' cloak, her pain might be relieved. What happens is an arresting response by Jesus himself, "who touched me?". Silly question according to those surrounding Jesus. What could they say? Crowds were milling around him. But Jesus himself gives an extraordinary answer: that he felt power going out of him, feeling drained in some way, his own life-power ebbing out of him, but life-giving, life-restoration to the suffering woman. She owns up. She has experienced the comfort of Jesus.

There are Gospel references to Jesus emotional, moved, sympathetic. Often quoted is his upset concern for the people, like sheep without a shepherd, distressed and desperate. One of the Google references expresses this beautifully, the Jesus did not just feel sorry, so to speak, but that his heart broke for them.

As Jesus frequently said, whoever sees me sees the Father. So, as we look at Jesus the comforter of the afflicted, we appreciate how much our God wants to comfort, not just to sympathise, but to empathise with what we are experience.

> Had not your law been my delight, I would have died in my affliction. (Psalm 118 – 119 – 89-96)

The pain may not be taken away, as we think of those with terminal illnesses, as we think of civilians bombed, hurt, in need of food and water, of those experiencing the pain of mental illness. But, please God, literally, we will find ways of comforting them.

Jesus Shelterer

The Psalms very frequently remind us, "God, in every age, you have been our refuge, our shelter".

An image comes to mind, that of Uluru, the heart centre of Australia, of walking around the vast monolith, observing the nooks and crannies, the sheltering clefts in the rock, the soothing pools of water at the base as we walk around in contemplation. God, our rock, refuge, shelter. And, in his time and, of course, now, Jesus is our refuge, our shelter. It is true that Jesus wept over Jerusalem and would have gathered the people together, sheltering them like a mother hen.

Shelter is not a word we use in connection with Jesus, Jesus Shelterer, but, in many ways, that is who he is, how he is our refuge.

Another image comes to mind, Jesus having pity on the crowds, seeing them bewildered, like sheep without a shepherd – and then his reaching out to them, reaching out as far as that one out of 100 sheep who was lost and is carried back safe, found.

We could make a list of those women and men who experienced Jesus as shelter. Here is my proposed (initial) list. You will have yours. And all of us will continue to add to our lists.

I would like to start with some of the women and discover why they found Jesus a shelter – and from whom they were taking shelter. The woman who always comes to my mind (reinforced by the seminars over the years of looking at the variety of many films over the decades which have dramatised this story). Yes, the woman to be first-stoned (John 8). She found shelter in Jesus not casting stones, comfort from the hounds of the law, stones at-the-ready. "No one accuses you" - after they slink away. "Neither do I" and she is safe and saved.

It is very much the same at Simon the Pharisees banquet, Luke 7:36-50, condemnation and disgust at the prostitute gatecrashing, tear-washing and anointing, rituals they had deliberately and slightingly omitted. Jesus says she is beloved and forgiven. Those observing were left with smug satisfaction in their law. And, of course, there is the woman at the well of Samaria (John 4) listened to, conversation welcomed, defended against criticism, even from Jesus disciples.

There is a constant need for shelter from judgemental attitudes stances, especially when righteousness appeals to the law for justification.

But, one episode where Jesus is spontaneous and sheltering grief is his encounter with the widow of Naim and giving her back her son. Mary of Bethany, listening at Jesus' feet is sheltered from her sister, Martha's worrying and fretting work-orientation complaints. But, Martha herself, lessons learned, finds shelter in grief in Lazarus's death, when Jesus affirms her faith in his risen life. And Jesus continues his sheltering of the sisters when Martha is back serving the meal to visitors and Mary anoints Jesus, and with lavish anointments. Jesus defends her against the double standards, those of Judas.

And some men? What of the leper who risked the restrictions of the law and hurried it to appeal, to touch Jesus and be welcomed and healed (Mark 1). And there is, of course, Zacchaeus (Luke 19), bidden by Jesus to come down from the shelter of the tree to entertain him at a meal and be sheltered by the gift of atonement. And the man born blind and healed (John 9), who was the victim of a false theology that said guilt is inherited, that punishment for sins of past generations is inherited and worn by an afflicted, innocent sufferer. (Yes we do inherit the consequences of sinful pasts and have to take some responsibilities for atonement, taking us beyond any self-centred tormented guilt feelings).

This brings this reflection to a pause, rather than an end. This time it is Calvary, Jesus sheltering the good thief who is dying with him, the shelter of Paradise that day. And, finally, shelter for Mary his mother, standing at the foot of the cross, her son cruelly taken from her, but ensuring that she be comforted (and a reminder of the moving scene from the television film, Jesus, 1999, Mary with the dead Jesus on her lap, *Pieta*, with Andrew Lloyd Webber's *Pie Jesu* in the background – followed then by a strong Mary leading the other women to the anointing of Jesus.)

It would be interesting/inspiring to see your list.

Jesus and the Grace of Endurance

"Your endurance will save you". These are the words of Jesus in Luke 19, after his rather fearful summing up of disasters and the worst of times. So, a prayer for the grace of endurance is prayer during the worst.

Endurance is not a word we necessarily associate with prayer. Do we speak of a "spirituality of endurance"? And what does endurance consist of? Some suggestions: faith, fidelity, constancy, trust, perseverance, persistence, outreach, compassion, empathy... Quite a comprehensive spirituality once this is expressed.

At the end of the Church's year, Ordinary Time, the winding down of the liturgical cycle before it opens up again with Advent, the Church asks us to reflect on hard times, especially in Year C, a focus on death, even martyrdom, life after death, and then the coming of what we might call apocalyptic horrors. And Jesus speaks on quite a world scale, from the destruction of the Temple in Jerusalem to natural disasters like earthquakes and drought, then more globally, so to speak, on wars, nations against nation – though he does finish on a personal scale with conflict in families, betrayals...

In wondering how to speak a homily on these readings, the thought occurred: if Jesus were standing at the lectern, speaking out this same message to a 21st-century community, what might he say? How specific would he be? (And, at the beginning of the homily, asking the congregation what they might imagine Jesus would say, situations that had made an impact on them in recent times.)

So, Jesus in the 2020s, his grim reflection on the times.

Perhaps to give a tone to what he wanted to say, he would go back to September 11, 2001, the visuals, so surprisingly, shockingly, there on our television screens, the planes flying into the World Trade Centre, 3000 deaths that day, so many injured, consequent deaths, and such grief and anguish. In a way, 9/11 ushered in the apocalyptic aspects of the 21st-century, wars, Afghanistan, invasion of Iraq and their consequences for so long.

And when Jesus referred to earthquakes and drought: close to home, Tonga experienced two earthquakes in 2022, the first leading to a tsunami. And 2023 began with enormous quakes and aftershocks in winter for Turkey and Syria. And, drought, familiar in Australia but a constant for many years in the countries of North East Africa, Somalia, Ethiopia. Jesus didn't mention bushfires and floods but we can. They are becoming more intense, more frequent, Australia experiencing devastating bushfires 2019-2020, and 2022 a year of continuous floods, month after month, town after town awash and then it happening over again, down the east coast of Australia, then in the Kimberleys, the north of the Northern Territory, then the Gulf of Carpentaria.

And wars? Nation against nation? Sudan, civil war in Yemen, military coup and oppression in Myanmar. The Russian invasion of Ukraine and the fightback. And the horrors of 2023, Israel and the Hamas massacre and hostages, then the long, fierce bombardment of Gaza, then Lebanon and the tens of thousands homeless, hungry, wounded, dead.

And, perhaps, the congregation in reflecting had their thoughts turning to the pandemic, Covid 19, the spread of the coronavirus and its variations, worldwide. The global experience of infection, illness, so many deaths. And the consequences in lockdown, isolation and separations, borders closed, travelling contact limited, touching everyone, and for so long. Looking back on 2020, the experience of lockdowns, and that year now seeming something of a black hole in our lives.

So much to endure.

But, Jesus knew what he was talking about in using the word endurance. We think of his agony in the Garden of Gethsemane, facing up to what was to come. There was endurance in his arrest, the insults of his trials, torment and torture, crucifixion – but, at the end, he was able to express the desire for pardon for those who had hurt him, was able to breathe forth his spirit, completing his mission with us on earth. And, there was Mary, his mother, standing in endurance at the foot of the cross.

And we remember that Jesus had great compassion for those whose illness made endurance demands on them, the woman with the haemorrhage for so many years, trusting desperately to touch the hem of his cloak, the man born blind and the ridicule and criticism by the religious leaders and the people, and all those, with the hope of the prophet Isaiah for that day of joy and healing, the blind, the deaf, the lame... And the empathetic Jesus literally reaching out to them, knowing their pain. (This might seem something of an anti-climax, but in the Gospel sparring with the Sadducees, religious leaders who refused to believe in the life after death, taunted Jesus with their hypothesis of the woman married to 7 husbands and her status in the afterlife, we are reminded that Jesus had to endure not only criticism but humiliating mockery – something which his followers in subsequent centuries have also had to endure for their faith.) A prayer for all times, a prayer for our times, Jesus, give us the grace of endurance.

No First Stone

Cast the first stone – and everybody knows what that means, it evokes the woman taken in adultery, the accusations of the religious leaders of Jesus' time, and Jesus' invitation/challenge to them to exercise their righteousness: cast the first stone. And that phrase is known well beyond Christianity.

In fact, Jesus tends to cast a lot of first stones, mainly against double standards, against hypocrisy, acknowledging that we should do what religious leaders urge us to do but not do what they themselves actually do. And Jesus also casts some rebuke-stones at his disciples, their doubts and their stupidities. But not when it came to those condemned as sinners, the woman at Simon's banquet, Luke 7, urging Zacchaeus to come down the tree, Luke 19, going to dine with tax collectors and prostitutes, Luke 15, leading to the parable of the prodigal son, and, of course, John 8 and the woman taken in the very act of committing adultery. Which does seem rather invasive and prurient legislation and policing. No wonder those eager to administer punishment were righteously ready, stones in hand, accusations clear, penalty exact.

While these leaders wanted to catch Jesus as a breaker of the Mosaic law, it would seem in these incidents that there was an implied guilt by association.

But, there is one film version of the story where Jesus does cast the first stone (to which he is entitled because he is without sin). It occurs rather surprisingly in the 1965 film, *The Greatest Story Ever Told*. That is the gospel film with a rather incongruous Jesus (though some might say that all the films with Jesus so European and white are incongruous), Jesus played by tall Swedish actor, Max von Sydow. No lightness of touch here. But, when challenged by the Pharisees, he holds out a stone in his hand for them to take it and throw. Then unexpectedly, Jesus flings the stone. Hard. Not at the woman - but away from her, at the ground. He is innocent so does not throw condemnatory and punitive stones.

This is an episode frequently presented in the movies, starting with *Intolerance* as early as 1916, repeated through the decades, culminating as part of the film version of the full text of John's Gospel in 2003, *The Gospel of John*. In looking at that film, traditionally presented, period, costumes, décor, a pleasingly humane Jesus, the episode is acted out while Canadian actor, Christopher Plummer, narrates the text with the comment by Jesus, the woman's reply, and Jesus urging her to go free and not sin again. Perhaps this is just as we might have imagined it as we listen to Gospel readings.

There is always the caution that too many have identified the woman taken in adultery with Mary Magdalene, imputing sexual misbehaviour to her because of her being healed from seven demons, mental and physical illness. In fact, with Max von Sydow, the woman is dressed in bright red, a scarlet woman.

An unexpected dramatic presentation of this episode can be seen in *The Last Temptation of Christ*, 1988, as Mary Magdalene dragged along the ground, pulled by her hair, thrust into the presence of Jesus. But those eager to punish her (and some rather prurient policing), case unheard, are already throwing the stones at her, and with quite some force. In fact, a stone is actually thrown at Jesus himself, definitely a guilt by association.

Not every film version includes Jesus writing in the sand. Quite striking is Jesus' shaming those standing alert with their stones, writing (in Hebrew letters), their sins as they skulk away. In *Last Temptation*, Jesus is verbal, rather than writing, challenging one of the men with his hypocritical life.

A much better interpretation is in the 1999 television film, *Jesus*, with a younger and benign Jeremy Sisto as Jesus. And this time, the woman is not identified with Mary Magdalene whom we initially see with a client, who asks what is going on when there is a disturbance and she watches the woman in adultery being pushed towards Jesus. Mary Magdalene, sexually identified as usual, observes Jesus with the woman, Jesus noticing her, inviting her to follow him. She begins to stand her ground, declaring that she was free. Jesus says that she is not free – but that she could be, urging her to follow him. Which, of course, she does, with great significance. Jesus doodles in the sand and we see the outline of the Christian symbol, icthus, fish.

One of the features that many observe in the Jesus films is Jesus' treatment of the woman. In the 1927 *King of Kings*, Jesus raises the woman up, gently touching her. In the 1999 Jesus, Jesus is virtually kneeling on the ground, looking up to the woman, no domination at all, eye contact, raising her up, smiling, and her response of smile as she goes free. Jesus has the last word, 'Go, and sin no more'.

Of course, there is still the question for us: do we identify fully with the woman as a sinner, then as accused, as absolved? And, are we as compassionate as Jesus? When did we last cast a first stone?

Jesus is asking us to put self-righteousness on hold (at least).

Mary Magdalene, I Don't Know How to Love Him

With this reflection, I'm going to try something which I wasn't anticipating. The focus is on Mary Magdalene. While I will look to the Gospel mentions of her, and to the characters with whom she is confused in interpretation, I have decided to look at the impact of three songs with Tim Rice's lyrics and Andrew Lloyd Webber's melodies in *Jesus Christ Superstar*.

I have to confess to something a devotion I have for *Jesus Christ Superstar*, especially the 1973 film version, with Yvonne Elliman singing the songs. As you read this reflection, it would be pleasing to be able to listen to the songs. Failing that, the lyrics of each song are readily available by Googling.

First of all, the explicit Gospel references to Mary Magdalene herself. She is first named at the beginning of chapter 8 of St Luke, along with the group of women who were disciples of Jesus and who accompanied Jesus and his disciples in their travels, caring for them. And, there is that (interpreted so derogatorily) information that Jesus had cast out seven devils from her. There is no sexual implication in Gospel stories of others who had devils cast out. It is the woman who inherits the slur.

Mary Magdalene is seen as one of the few faithful disciples on Calvary, at the foot of the cross with Mary and the beloved disciple and Mary of Clopas. Her role is one of presence, one of support.

But, Mary Magdalene comes into her own with her experience of the resurrection. It is she, rather than the apostles, who ventures out to visit the tomb. It is she who discovers that Jesus is not there. It is she Jesus encounters, dispelling her concerns, calling her by name (as he did with the other apostles), urging her not to try to keep hold of him because he had to go to the Father. "You have to let me go." Mary races back to the upper room, becomes the apostle of the good news of Jesus resurrection, testifies to Jesus the Risen Lord. She is the one who enables the apostles to come out of themselves, out of their fears, and for Peter and John to hurry to the tomb – and to acknowledge that everything was as she had said. Mary Magdalene is one of the key figures of the resurrection narratives.

Because of the sexual interpretation of the seven devils cast out from her, tradition has Mary Magdalene associated with prostitution, especially with the woman in Luke 7:36-50, who is described as a woman who was a sinner in the city. She is a repentant prostitute. Franco Zeffirelli does this in his Jesus of Nazareth. She weeps her sorrow and repentance on Jesus' feet. And she pours ointment on them. The judgmental host, Simon, and guests are quick to condemn Jesus for this association and seem to be appalled that she is beloved and forgiven, something, they say, only God could do. (Or, others considering this more favourably, are amazed that Jesus is forgiving, something which God does.)

The anointing leads us to yet another Mary, Mary of Bethany, hosted Jesus with Martha and Lazarus, lamenting her brother's death and witnessing his coming to life again, present at the banquet where many from Jerusalem came to marvel, and Mary anoints Jesus' feet, receiving the rebuke from Judas about the money not being given to the poor, and Jesus counter rebuke that the poor are always with us but he himself will not be.

No, I have not forgotten the superstar songs. But, this is the context.

I would listen to Everything is All Right as the song of Mary's ministry of service and support.

> Try not to get worried, try not to turn onto
> Problems that upset you
> Don't you know
> Everything's alright, yes, everything's fine
> And we want you to sleep well tonight
> Let the world turn without you tonight
> If we try, we'll get by
> So forget all about us tonight.

Within the song there is the challenge from Judas about the money for the poor, as well as the answer from Jesus praising her anointing.

> And it's cool and the ointment's sweet
> For the fire in your head and feet.

Jesus, soothed, is to close his eyes and sleep.

Between the time that Mary Magdalene joins the group travelling with Jesus and her being present on Calvary, one can speculate of the effect of Jesus on her, in terms of faith and commitment, in terms of hope and his achievement, in terms of love and how it affects her personally, in her heart.

Which is the cue for "I don't know how to love him",

> I don't know how to love him
> What to do, how to move him
> I've been changed yes really changed
> In these past few days when I've seen myself
> I seem like someone else

The lyrics of the song do presuppose Mary and her prostitute past, her experience of men, her bewilderment in the presence of Jesus, how she should react with him, fear, love. Tim Rice has created an unexpected love song. This has driven Mary and her discipleship, to her presence at the foot of the cross.

However, Rice and Lord Webber have another song involving Mary. This time she sings it with Peter, a repentant Peter, watching Jesus as he goes towards his passion, wishing to save him, "Could we start again, please"?

> I think you've made your point now
> You've even gone a bit too far to get the message home
> Before it gets too frightening, we ought to call a halt
> So could we start again please?

In fact, this yearning in Mary, the surprise of the passion, her being present at Jesus' death, leads to a starting again that she could not have anticipated, discovering that he had risen and being the first to proclaim it.

Jesus Lifted up, Drawing us to Himself

Do you have a favourite crucifixion image? Perhaps favourite is not quite the apt word for such a choice. Our image might be Calvary, the three crosses silhouetted against the darkening sky, Mary, Mary Magdalene and John at the foot of the cross. Or, we might favour a close-up of Jesus crucified, what people generally mean when they say, crucifix. Or, mission achieved, the peaceful face of Jesus who has died for us. On a personal level, I very much like the Pieta, and the film version of it in the 1999 Jesus, Mary holding her dead son in her lap, quiet grief, Jesus at last at peace, and the background of Andrew Lloyd Webber's *Requiem*.

But, I wish I were creative artist. I would like to have an image of the crucifixion according to Jesus' words, "when I am lifted up, I will draw all people to myself" (John 12:32). And, symbolically, in John 3, Jesus quotes a precedent to Nicodemus, God's people suffering in the desert (Numbers), the snakes, and Moses then lifting up his staff, urging everyone to look, to look up, with faith and hope, to be healed.

Which means then that my image of the crucifix would somehow portray Jesus nailed, his hands nailed, but, at the same time, the fingers bent, reaching outwards towards everyone, a combination of his urging, his calling, his invitation, to not be afraid and to confidently come towards him as he gives his life for us.

In John 12, when Jesus refers to his being lifted up and drawing everyone to himself, he then adds that, at this moment, everyone will know that "I am...". So, this outreach of Jesus, lifted up on the cross, drawing us all, is meant to be a revelation of who he is and, not only who he is, but inviting us into a new awareness of the mystery of the Father, seeing Jesus like this on the cross, seeing a fullness-of-love God. And we remember, of course, the revelation to Moses at the burning bush, the God who reveals the divine name, I am, I am who I am, the living God (Exodus 4).

We might remember that Jesus spoke a number of 'I am' revelations throughout John's Gospel: Bread of Life (he would also give us living water), Light of the world, Good Shepherd, Resurrection and the life, True Vine – and the Way, the Truth and the Life.

So, how to get all this into the one crucifixion picture. I would welcome a creative artist – but the image is there in our hearts, in our minds, in our imaginations.

This was reinforced unexpectedly when I was invited to the press preview of a film called *Father Stu*, the one about the boxer played convincingly by Mark Wahlberg, in his young, rather ordinary worldly days, a drifter, who eventually became a priest. Actually, while watching it in the early sequences, immersed in the rather rough and ready world, no spirituality around, I was dubious about how this life could possibly lead to vocation and ordination. Would this be one of those somewhat preachy faith-based films that Americans like? A preachy parable? Ultimately, it was more convincing, happily, than I expected, conversion, credible, a spirituality, a decision to become a priest, the years of training, illness and testing, ministry.

The connection with this reflection – at the core of Stu's religious experience was a severe car accident, his Damascus moment one might say, a sense of Mary present comforting him, but also, his listening to a Hispanic priest speaking about the crucifixion and suffering. Stu had to endure more, a debilitating muscular disease. But, what comes to my memory is Stu, always a down-to-earth speaker, even in his homilies, energising the congregation about Jesus suffering on the cross, Stu standing by a crucifix in the church, making us realise that if we are to understand and value the suffering in our life, it can only be done by our sharing Jesus' suffering and death. Jesus knows, to the extreme, what human suffering is like. He lived and died it.

There is some discussion in the film about God and the problem of evil, God allowing evil and suffering, permitting it, not intervening – but, that is a philosophical and analytical theological discussion, sometimes moving a grieving and angry situation into abstract argument. Stu reminds us that we need to be real, to look at Jesus, to identify Jesus, in his suffering, where he identifies with us. Stu is right. He experienced Jesus lifted up, drawing Stu to himself, Stu recognising who Jesus is, seeing Jesus on the Cross – and seeing in Jesus, the Father.

Jesus, his Bequest, his new Commandment

This was not a planned *10 Minutes* reflection. Rather, it came about from preparing a homily, for the 5th Sunday of Easter Gospel, where, at the end of the Last Supper, in the spirit of his washing the Apostles' feet, Jesus offered his bequest, his legacy, by which they would be recognised as his disciples, the new commandment of loving one another as he loved us.

The idea behind the homily was the producing of a television documentary show, akin to the ABC's *Tomorrow Tonight*, a panel which discusses issues from a variety of points of view. So, points of view on Jesus' legacy.

The first invitee would be someone whose philosophy of life was completely secular, living in this world which is the totality of existence. Nothing transcendent. Nothing beyond. This is the stance of the men and women who want to do their best in life. But our invitee would have developed a hostile attitude towards Jesus, and especially hostility towards what they see him representing in the history of Christianity. Jesus would be seen as a figurehead for so much bigotry, persecution, negative influence in our world.

What came to mind was the Agony in the Garden scene in the 1999 television film, *Jesus*. Satan appears in a dapper black suit, trying to undermine Jesus' faith in his father, taking him back through history, watching the Crusaders riding into battle, wielding swords, crying out in the name of Jesus; Satan then delays in Inquisition times watching a witch being burnt, the mitred and crozier-wielding Bishop proclaiming that this execution was in the name of Jesus, purifying the Church; then Satan walks Jesus through the ruins and trenches of World War I... Satan showing Jesus what would be perpetrated in his name.

The second invitee would be a staunch Christian, not so much a person of faith but, rather, a person of strong beliefs, convinced that Jesus spoke the truth, of the unshakeable conviction that this truth would set us free. This is calling on the name of Jesus for self-righteous behaviour, imposition of Jesus' law, the letter of the law rather than any investigation of the spirit of the law. Perhaps this is the attitude of the Bishop in that Agony in the Garden sequence just mentioned – perhaps it is the crusader for orthodoxy Christian, fiercely literal and fundamentalist.

But the third invitee – and one hopes that we might be invited because we fall (no, stand tall) into this category – is the person who knows that the truth of the Law is love of God and love of neighbour, and not just in any abstract sense, but in following the example of Jesus, servant/slave washing of feet service for others, which means 'every other', and laying down one's day-to-day life, even laying down one's life in death as he did, so that everyone can see what Jesus was like, who Jesus was, by everyone seeing and appreciating the inheriting Jesus' legacy of love and putting it into practice.

After the homily, one of the congregation suggested that I should have invited another member to the panel, a mystic. This is the disciple who not only imitates Jesus in action, but lives, fully, in Jesus, communicating with him, bringing the deep intimacy of love and prayer into service, living contemplation in action. The suggestion was not only good, it was profound. (Definitely next time.)

It is easy to pay lip-service to Jesus' command, to bask, at times, in the glow of seeing how much good others do in Jesus' name. And we should be joyful when we see the small day-to-day kindnesses, when we hear of the massive efforts on individuals and charities to reach out to those bereft of comforts that we take for granted, let alone the necessities of life. And we can be reminded of the selflessness of the Good Samaritan. But we need to read, often, to the end of Jesus' telling this story to the religious interpreter of the law who had, perhaps defensively, demanded of Jesus, "and who is my neighbour?". And when Jesus parried the question with another question, and the lawyer came up with the correct answer, Jesus was very direct, even blunt, to him – and to us – "Go and do the same yourself.".

Gethsemane Moments

Jesus identified with us. We are all invited to identify with him.

We can say that God knows intimately everything we experience, especially in the testing, trying, suffering times of our lives. God in Jesus has shared our experiences, shared in our experiences, has complete empathy with us. When we suffer or grieve, we can bring to our consciousness the moment when Jesus suffered or grieved. One of the key images of these moments is the agony in the garden, Jesus facing the reality of his suffering and death, full of dread, asking the Father that he could be released from this fate, overwhelmed, but, acceptance, determination, the will to live through whatever was to come, even death.

It seems important for us to be aware of our own Gethsemane moments. And to look back at some of Jesus' other experiences, Gethsemane-like moments, and for us to identify with them.

A friend told me recently that in her down moments, she was miserable. In his moments did Jesus feel miserable? I never heard that in a Litany, Jesus most miserable, have mercy on us. But, it's worth reflection. Jesus miserable – in Gethsemane especially, lonely, feeling abandoned, fearful, anxious, afraid of the worst come. It is an invitation to us in our own Gethsemane moments to identify with Jesus miserable – but Jesus did not stay miserable, did not wallow in his misery. He prayed and the chalice did pass him by, giving him courage, strength to go on. And, a reminder that through Jesus God can be vulnerable – and miserable.

Some moments. After the manifestation of his mission in the baptism by John in the Jordan, Jesus went through his testing experience, the 40 days echo of the 40 years of Israel in the desert-Exodus before reaching the promised land, dramatised by Matthew and Luke as three temptations/testings. Jesus is hungry, weak, experiencing uncertainty, but with each moment of testing, he becomes stronger, defying this spirit-not-of-God, in the words of the Psalm being "calm but vigilant", emerging from the torment of these Gethsemane moment tests, to conviction, to strong will, to new purpose in his commitment to his ministry.

To take another quite different experience: Jesus' empathy with those grieving for the deaths of loved ones. Jesus had Gethsemane moments with the widow from Naim, spontaneously stopping when he caught sight of the funeral procession. Pausing with her, distressed, conscious of mortality – but with the gift of offering her son to her with renewed life. It was the same with Mary and Martha so sad at the death of their brother Lazarus and Jesus not coming to heal him as he died. And that famous verse from John, "Jesus wept". And, again, a gift of renewed life. Jesus' Gethsemane moments included his human sadness, emotional grief, but with confidence that there could be new and renewed life.

There is a complete contrast in Jesus' Gethsemane moments with the enormous amount of criticism that he received, especially from the religious leaders, the scribes and Pharisees, always on the alert to catch him, to trick him, to denounce him, to complain continually. He was their target. These are the Gethsemane moments of frustration. And they had, at times, a powerful effect on Jesus. Just think of his denunciations in Matthew 23, no hesitation in his rhetoric against the whitened sepulchres... But, calmly realising that, with their authority, they should be listened to but not followed because they do not practice what they preach. Even when Jesus is brought before Annas, the high priest, denounced, spat on, his beard pulled, his rebuke, tested by three years of insults, is only the quiet question.

At times Jesus' Gethsemane moments were with his own disciples, Even with the Twelve, frustrations with Peter and his moments of incomprehension, even to betrayal, the questions after the Last Supper and Jesus regretful, "how long have I been with you...?" Gethsemane moments which had to lead to day-by-day patience, some tolerance, some appreciation and understanding of his followers' limitations.

But, the Gethsemane moment was in the garden itself, his prayer, the prayer for deliverance, the human sadness of the incomprehension of the apostles, his 'support group' failing, fleeing, the sleeping of his favoured three even, as the Gospel says, his sweat was anxious blood. These Gethsemane moments were his most harrowing, God's human realisation that he must undergo extreme experiences of suffering, and extreme, lonely and isolating, death.

Which means that Jesus final Gethsemane moments were on the cross. After betrayal, arrest, hostile cross-examination, whipping, crown of thorns, mockery, carrying the cross, lifted high alone (and between thieves), the final desperation, "oh God, why have you forsaken me...?". But, through that final desperation emerged human heroism, graced Gethsemane moments, the possibility for forgiving those who had destroyed him, bonding his mother and the disciple and the prayer that we pray will be ours in every Gethsemane moment, large or small in our lives, but in our death, "Lord, into your hands, I commend my spirit".

Jesus, God's Final Word

Over the decades, I had read this excerpt from the Office of Readings, Monday, Advent week 2, but this time, I was stirred. Jesus as God's final word.

> 'When God gave us, as he did, his Son, who is his one Word, he spoke everything to us, once and for all in that one Word. There is nothing further for him to say'. John of the Cross, *The Ascent of Mount Carmel*, Book 2, Chapter 22.

The key New Testament text:

> At various times in the past and in various different ways, God spoke to our ancestors through the prophets; but in our own time, in the last days, he has spoken to us through his Son [Hebrews 1:1-2].

Which means, of course, that if we listen to what Jesus said and look at what he did, we see God. And that is what Jesus keeps reminding his disciples, especially in John's Gospel, whoever sees me sees the Father. The Father and I are one.

A valuable exercise for our appreciating our seeing and hearing God through Jesus would be to list our favourite sayings of Jesus, his actions that we most appreciate.

Here is something of a personal list. You will have yours.

If I want to hear what God values, then I listen to the Beatitudes, especially the familiar version from Matthews's Sermon on the Mount. God's highest ideals for living love of God and love of our neighbour. And, staying with Matthew, I value the welcoming, "Come to me, all you who labour...". We are to appreciate the heart of God in Jesus, gentle and humble, where we will find rest.

And those God-images in Jesus' parables in Luke, the prodigal father who allows his wayward son to make his own choices, to ruin his life if he wished, but who was loving, prodigal in welcoming when his son returned, rejoicing that the son who is dead has come to life. And there is his wish that his dour elder son, whom he reminds that everything the father has is his, to appreciate the joy of repentance and change of heart. There is also the Good Samaritan, rescuing and bandaging the injured "enemy" and ensuring that he would be cared for. God extravagantly loving, tenderly caring.

And, there is a wonderful three-word translation of Jesus' response to the woman, adulterous yes, but dragged humiliatingly before him so that the religious authorities could judge him righteous in the eyes of the law - and cast the first stone at her. When he asks the woman who is condemning her and she replies that there is no one, they have all skulked away, he proclaims the wonderful reassurance "neither do I".

I experienced a distraction when trying to note what actions of Jesus I would select. Suddenly, I thought of the popular novel and film, *Eat, Love, Pray*. It does provide helpful Gospel headings!

I like and enjoy the fact that Jesus was comfortable in having meals, the social and sociable God. He was certainly happy at the house of Martha, Mary and Lazarus, twice. He and the apostles were happy to be ministered to, meals prepared, by the group of women who followed them in their travels, especially Mary Magdalene. And, of course, there is his "divine decision" to have meals with fraudulent money collectors and prostitutes. Most notably, dining with Zacchaeus.

Comparisons are made with John the Baptist and Jesus was referred to as a glutton and a wine-bibber. So we can wonder why

Simon the Pharisee actually invited him to a meal, not offering him the customary ritual cleansing courtesies, and the meal developing into controversy about who can forgive sins, Jesus identifying with the father in this case, and able to reassure that the woman who had gatecrashed the party that she was beloved and forgiven. In the eating stories, Jesus manifested God's loving friendship as well as God's reconciliation outreach.

And for Jesus loving in action, we all have our favourite stories where Jesus encounters someone, especially the poor, especially those who need healing, his sensitivity to the woman with the haemorrhage, his gentleness with Jairus's daughter resuscitated, the woman at the well in Samaria, and his treatment of his close friends, the apostles, especially his patient putting up with Peter and his impetuousness.

For Jesus' action in praying, we remember that he withdrew from his friends, from the crowds, to spend time in union with the father, in prayer. But, what I like to contemplate is his prayer and action in his suffering and death, his uncertainties, fear and sweating blood in Gethsemane, the taunts at his trials, scourging and crowning thorns mockery, carrying the cross to Calvary, execution between thieves, death and breathing forth his spirit and his side pierced.

This is what God chose and consented to, divine action in lived human experience, from birth to death, the ordinary day-by-day events, but the divine willingness, ultimately, to experience the extremes of utter loneliness, deep feelings of abandonment, and accepting physical and mental pain – to the utmost.

In his suffering and death, Jesus shows us that God has experienced whatever any of us as human beings have experienced or will experience. Our suffering – God knows.

But, in Jesus' death and his final yes to the father, the Father completely accepts this willing incarnation of Jesus. Human experience – even to the extremes – is not alien to God and its fulfilment will be joy of risen life.

Christ Reigns

At the end of the Church's liturgical calendar, we find something of a culmination of all that we have lived through, the Feast of Christ the King. It used to be celebrated in October, many of us making our First Communion on that day, back in the good old days! In recent decades, this focus on Christ the King has been triumphant.

However, when we listen to one of the Gospels for the feast, from John 18:36, we hear Jesus say to Pontius Pilate that "my kingdom is not of this world". It is in no sense of a worldly kingdom. There is an even more striking assertion of who Jesus was as king in another Gospel for the feast, this time from Luke. Pilate had commanded the notice be placed on the cross, the King of the Jews. While Jesus was mocked by the crowds and one of the thieves, the other asked Jesus' pardon and was promised a place in that other kingdom, the paradise of the faithful.

In its origins, this feast of Christ the King was to be a counterbalance to worldly ambitions. Perhaps you did not realise that the feast was instituted not so long ago, within the last century, 1925. Pius XI was dismayed by the rise of Mussolini in Italy, fascist government, fascist behaviour, a "worldly" oppressive mentality. Pius XI gave this feast to the universal church as a protest, a stance against fascist kingdoms. And, this was to be significant in the coming years with the rise of Hitler and the Third Reich, the hubris of a 1000 year worldly rule of racist domination.

But, with the defeat of Hitler, with the end of World War II, kingdoms were disappearing or they survived mainly with ceremonial status. The era of kings and kingdoms was coming to an end. Which makes the title, Christ the King, though scripturally based, somewhat anachronistic. And, with the consciousness of inclusive language, kingdom has overtones of the male ruler.

This has been the experience of Britain and Commonwealth countries in 2022 with the death of Queen Elizabeth. We have had so long to wait for Charles to become king, have seen him so much on the media, know so much about him, that it is difficult to use the title, Majesty, for him. Monarchs in recent decades have become less majestic.

Which is why this chapter is entitled Christ Reigns. It is more inclusive in its tone. And it translates the Latin, regnum, more obviously. (But, long tradition will keep us praying in the Our Father, thy kingdom come.)

Another historical aside. Australians, whether it be in their colonial history or in the Federation/Commonwealth, have generally been ruled by Queens rather than Kings. Queen Victoria had 64 years, 1837-1901. Queen Elizabeth II had 70 years and counting, 1952-2022. Which seems to leave only 1901-1952 when Australia was ruled by Kings, five of them in that period!

It might be helpful to go back to the Jewish Scriptures and the attitude of Israel towards Kings. Initially, the prophet Samuel as leader and judge, was against Israel having a king. The Lord was King. And this language continued through the Psalms, "the Lord is King with majesty enrobed...". But, when Samuel finally relented, interpreting God's will, the Hebrew king would always be subordinate to the Lord. When Saul overstepped these boundaries, he was dismissed. David and his descendants were second to the Lord as King, David the shepherd, even when many of them overstepped with their ambitions, so that when, finally, the people went into exile, the monarchy disappeared.

In Jesus' time, matters were worse, an empire, a dominating Emperor.

But, back to John 19, the kind of kingdom that is not of this world and which, in the Our Father, we pray for, is the kingdom which Paul describes (Galatians 5:22-23) "the kingdom of God, and what this Spirit brings is very different: love, joy, peace, patience, kindness, goodness, trustworthiness, gentleness and self-control... It is like a treasure hidden in a field, a pearl of great price, a tiny mustard seed that grows into the greatest of shrubs, where justice and peace reign, where justice and mercy prevail, forgiveness seventy times seven and beyond, where love of God and neighbour is the hallmark, where this kind of love fulfils the whole law.

And, while this reign is not of this world, it is here on earth, with a faith and commitment to God's word, with trust and hope in God's continuing covenant, and with love that never ends.

At the end of liturgical year, on the feast, we celebrate how Christ Reigns.

Mary's Advent

During the Advent season we are longing, urged to long, for the coming of Jesus, the beginnings of his sharing our human lives with us. However, with the fourth Sunday of Advent, the Gospels focus on his mother, Mary.

Which means we are invited to reflect on what Advent was for Mary, Mary's Advent.

In fact, of course, her Advent was nine months, her pregnancy. The early Christian communities, especially those of Matthew and Luke, reflected, imagined, speculated, created stories of what her pregnancy meant to Mary. And they drew on the traditions of the Jewish Scriptures, the prophetic tradition, the anticipation of the coming of the saviour, and the images of mothers in that tradition. As we know from Jesus' own visits to the synagogues, his proclaiming the Scriptures in Nazareth, Mary went to the synagogue, heard the prophecies.

The one that appealed to Matthew's community was that of Isaiah 7, of the maiden being with child, giving birth to her son, Emanuel, God is with us. The Matthew community saw this as a fulfilment text. But, with Luke's community, and the focus on Jesus as a hero, many strains of the Jewish Scriptures were interwoven in the story of the Annunciation, Jesus as the son of David, King David, announced by the prophet of the fulfilment of time, Gabriel, the language of the spirit of God. And the maiden, with child, said simply that she was the handmaid of the Lord.

The Matthew community saw it is God's plan that she should be betrothed to the good and just man, Joseph, and live her life at Nazareth during her pregnancy. They also saw the religious and social difficulties of the unmarried pregnant young woman. According to the law, she would be accused of adultery, taken out for stoning. It came as something of a shock to some of us in the 1970s when an American television movie, *Mary and Joseph*, actually dramatised this for us. The townspeople were angry, ready with rocks. But Mary was rescued. And Joseph, seemingly badly embarrassed by this potential scandal, decided to put her aside. He did not want to cast the first stone. His decision to support Mary and become the foster father of her child was part of the tradition of dreams, that of Joseph, son of Jacob, who discerned God's will through dreams.

But, in the imagination of Luke's community, Mary did not stay all the time in Nazareth. One of the Gospels of the fourth Sunday of Advent is that of the Visitation, Mary taking the sometimes-precarious journey from Galilee down to Judaea, to visit her cousin, Elizabeth. That is the occasion, of course, for the creation of the first part of the favourite prayer, *Ave Maria/Hail Mary*. Because the Gospel had created a story of an Annunciation to Elizabeth' husband, Zachariah, visited by the angel Gabriel with the message of Elizabeth's unexpected pregnancy, her child John, the links made between the two cousins and their two sons – John, who would announce Jesus, gleeful in the womb at the presence of Jesus, leaping for joy.

There was also the wonderful link between Jesus, son of David, and John, like the prophet Samuel who would anoint David as king. Samuel was also an unexpected child and his mother, Hannah, is graced with a joyful Canticle in 1 Samuel. But, this time it is Mary who sings the Canticle, rejoicing in God, gracious and his lifting her up, a figure of great reverence, veneration. The Magnificat.

The Litany of Loreto, the Marian Litany, is not so well-known as it was in the past. One of the invocations was Ark of the Covenant,

Pray for us. The suggestion was this: the Ark of the covenant, containing the 10 Commandments, and considered the resting and dwelling place of God's presence, travelled around, reverenced by all. And, so, the suggestion is that Mary visiting Elizabeth and having the effect on John in Elizabeth's womb, was the equivalent of the grace-travels of the Ark.

The Matthew and Luke communities were very creative, always with reference to the scriptural traditions, in telling the Advent stories of Mary. One of the advantages of our media-image world is that filmmakers also exercise their imaginations. This is the point where I should mention the 2006 film, The Nativity Story. The writers keep their eye on the Gospels but imagine what Mary's day-to-day life was at home, family, her work, friends, her young age, the physical demands of her pregnancy, what we might call also the psychological demands. Especially recommended is the sequence where Mary and Joseph travel from Nazareth to Bethlehem. We might not have given much thought to what this was like, but a 100 km journey, from Galilee, through the mountains of Samaria, to the high country of Judaea, to over-crowded Bethlehem. Journeying by day, camping by night, Mary riding the donkey, Joseph and his leading her, and Mary coming to term for the impending birth.

Of course, that journey may not have been exactly like that in the film – but, on the other hand, it might have been.

And, so to Bethlehem, exertions, Joseph and his care, Mary and the continuing mystery of her pregnancy – and yet the ordinariness, with the Gospels going beyond the ordinary, stable, manger, cattle, shepherds (many of whom were rogues, stealing sheep rather than statues in a crib), the Magi, and angels singing. And we have so many Christmas carols and melodies to reinforce this.

But, life for Mary and Joseph and the baby Jesus didn't stay in the crib and stable. There was more to come, the fierceness of Herod, the persecution of and deaths of the children, flight into Egypt and life in exile, refugees.

Both dramatic and what we might call devotional, Mary's Advent.

Joseph, the Wise and Just Man

It seems better to highlight this reflection on Joseph with an emphasis on his being wise and just. Rather than simply heading it, St Joseph. Which is a challenge to how we imagine, how we think about St Joseph. Is he an image, picture, a holy card, a statue, present in the crib? How real is he? How real does he seem to be?

One way of checking on this is to Google St Joseph/images. And, there he is, sometimes very old and bearded, venerable, sometimes middle-aged, in his carpentry workshop, sometimes rather younger, vigorous, with Jesus as an apprentice, or protecting Mary, or part of the Holy Family. Sometimes these pictures are "realistic". At other times they are quite "stylised". And there seemed to be an increasing number of icons.

For a long time, St Joseph had his feast day on March 19. In the middle of the 20th century, Pope Pius XII instituted the feast of St Joseph the Worker, May 1st, a Catholic counterbalance for May Day with its traditional European socialist celebrations. And, for 2021, Pope Francis nominated the year as the year of St Joseph. In my religious congregation, there has been the 19th century tradition from the founder, Jules Chevalier, to refer to St Joseph as "Model and Patron of those who love the Sacred Heart".

Which takes us back to the sources of any knowledge of Joseph. The principal sources, of course, are the infancy narratives in

Matthew and Luke and the later references in Matthew 13:55 and Mark 6:3, in Matthew the reference to Jesus as the carpenter's son, in Mark the reference to Jesus as the carpenter.

However, the Jewish scriptural tradition absorbed into the Infancy narratives has top priority. And it is from these that we can refer to Joseph, as does the preface for his feast day, as the wise and just man.

Which means then he is the line of exemplary fathers from the Wisdom Literature. It is the role of the wise father to instruct, to give example, to encourage and foster his children. Although the word "foster" is not used in the infancy narratives, we see how Joseph did foster Jesus, taking him to safety and exile in Egypt and then returning to Nazareth, sharing in the Nazareth responsibilities for Jesus as he grew up, dramatised by Luke with the story of the loss of Jesus in Jerusalem and his being found in discussion with the religious leaders, then returning home for a long fostering period before his public ministry. The story has Jesus at the age of 12, the age of the Jewish boy preparing for his Bar Mitzvah, learning the Scriptures, practising to proclaim them (and the adult Jesus noted by Luke as going to the synagogue in Nazareth and reading, as he was accustomed to, Jesus well-trained in these traditions).

And Luke's statement after Mary and Joseph found Jesus in Jerusalem and the interchange about his religious responsibilities to God, which baffle them at the time, Jesus went back home and was obedient to them, exemplary in the tradition of the Wisdom literature and its focus on the well-ordered and devout family. As the prayer for the feast of St Joseph says, 'Watchful care'.

Which does give us a moment to consider Joseph as a carpenter, working in trade, hard work, and artisan, a craftsman. And, the seeming assumption behind the references in Matthew and Mark suggest that Jesus himself worked with Joseph over those many years.

One of the effects of that fostering, with Mary mothering, is that Jesus learnt his human language from them as he grew up, eventually finding human language to help us to pray to God, the text of the Our Father.

The Jewish Scriptures wise and just man tradition also goes back to Genesis, to Joseph's namesake, Joseph, son of Jacob, a man with whom God communicated by dreams, imaginative night visions of what might be, both good and bad, and who acted on these dreams, saving the people of Egypt, and becoming the saviour of his father and brothers after his brothers' betrayal of him. It is in Matthew's infancy narratives that Joseph dreams, the key dream of his dilemma in the betrothal to Mary, her pregnancy, the potential for shame (even public stoning), and his decision to be her protector, leading him to be the foster father of her child, and the protection in exile, the God-communication by dream to escape to Egypt and, at Herod's death, to return to Nazareth.

Looking again at the Google selection of images of St Joseph, we realise that there can be a continual challenge to create images that reflect the whole scriptural tradition – and we are reminded that in the many Jesus movies, Joseph is brought to life, sometimes piously, sometimes vigorously and a recommendation for the Joseph of the 1999, Jesus, with Jeremy Sisto as Jesus and an older Armin Mueller-Stahl as Joseph; and another recommendation for *The Nativity Story* (2006), also recommended in the reflection on Mary's Advent, with Oscar Isaac as Joseph, details of life at Nazareth during Mary's pregnancy, and his protective accompanying her on the arduous journey, she nine months pregnant, from Nazareth to Bethlehem.)

And, as foster father and being of the line of David, going to the census in Bethlehem, Joseph provides the human legal lineage for Jesus as Son of David, successor to David, fulfilling all the promises made to David.

Profiling Peter's Faith Journey (Assisted by Carl Jung)

One of the features of the Gospel narratives is the outlining of various faith journeys. That of Martha is one of the most vivid. And there is a chapter here on the faith journey of Thomas. But the Gospel character, apart from Jesus himself, of course, who has the most extensive faith journey is Simon Peter.

We might think of his first meeting with Jesus and his being named Cephas, the Rock. We see him fishing at the Sea of Galilee, declaring himself a sinner, but immediately deciding to follow Jesus – and the bonus of the meal from his healed mother-in-law. He is present at the Transfiguration, at the raising of Jairus' daughter. He has questions about giving up everything and following Jesus, "what about us?". And "where else would we go, you have the words of eternal life?". And, of course, he is praised for his confession of Jesus as the son of the living God, responding to the Father's inspiration. But, when he expresses his fear of Jesus suffering, he is rebuked, a tempter, "get behind me, Satan". And then, he is sent to find the fish with the coin for the tax to Caesar. He promises loyal following but is told that he will deny Jesus three times. Deprecating, he does not want Jesus to wash his feet but, on hearing how necessary this is, he wants a complete body-wash. He does deny Jesus. He cowers in the upper room at the time of the crucifixion and afterwards. But he does run to see the empty tomb. Peter does have his great moment, expressing his faith and love in Jesus, three times, and given the wonder of a second chance, Feed my lambs, feed my sheep.

These are wonderful elements to ponder on. They constitute a portrait of Peter (to be affirmed by his activity at the time of Pentecost, preaching in Jerusalem, moving beyond Jerusalem, but still having to learn, that the pagans, like Cornelius, could be authentic disciples, challenged by Paul, the two significant letters from the early church attributed to him.) Profiling is a different matter, a way of understanding the character from the portrait. How might we profile and understand Peter?

He is very much a man who lives in his present, at home in the here and now, going out fishing, hard work, bringing in the fish, sorting the fish. Then he is so absorbed in the Transfiguration experience he wants to stay there, offering to build some tents. He is not a particularly subtle man. He has a straightforward loyalty, but in difficulties, he stumbles and denies Jesus. And, with the news of Jesus' resurrection, he does not simply accept the women's words, but has to run to the tomb, to see and check the reality for himself. He lives in the now/here, the reality of the present. Carl Jung would call this Sensing experience. Peter is not a man of possibilities or, as Jung says, Intuitions.

Peter is a brash man. He can be quick and decisive, not waiting to find out more information before he goes into action. He is quite definite and quick in leaving his boats behind him. He decides to follow Jesus and sticks to it, despite his putting his foot in it, told off as well as praised by Jesus, impetuous decisive, one might say, in wanting Jesus to wash him completely at the Last Supper – and then, in Gethsemane, a surprise when we remember that he is a fisherman, but his drawing a sword (that seemed to have come out of nowhere, Peter actually carrying sword and scabbard) and cutting off the ear of the high priest's servant. Peter is highly emotional, of course, but has solid Thinking grounds for his decisions.

It would seem that Peter, according to the Gospels, is not a very interior person, though his has his moments when inspired by the

Father to proclaim Jesus. Peter is more outgoing, more extroverted than introverted.

The Gospels are faith documents, not psychological studies. However, psychological insights can help us to appreciate, to understand something of the Gospel characters. But his final appearance in the Gospels, in John 21, after the practical fishing and eating the breakfast that Jesus had prepared on the shore of the Sea of Galilee, Peter has his high moment, an opportunity for confessing failings, declaration of love and loyalty, and his being rewarded by Jesus who names him, recognises him, appoints him, as pastoral leader.

We next hear of Peter in his courageous preaching of the Gospel in the Acts of the Apostles. That scene at the Sea of Galilee was a worthy end and a new beginning.

(PS. If any of you who are reading this have an appreciation for Katherine Briggs and Isabel Myers applications of Carl Jung's ideas, you might see Peter as ESTJ, and that style of leadership. On the other hand, you might have some different interpretations, fair enough.)

Thomas, According to the Gospel

In recent decades, with programs and speculations about apocryphal Gospels and their ideas, the 1945-rediscovered The Gospel of Thomas, along with the stories of his travels to India, have sometimes clouded over the actual story of Thomas, according to the Gospels, especially the Gospel of John.

A recommended Gospel quest is to single out a significant character from the Gospels, check the references, check their appearances, their words and actions, and see if a faith-journey can be traced. In the chapter on Jesus' Friends in *10 Minutes*, I did this rather quickly with Martha. She makes three appearances in the Gospels, two highly significant. Our introduction to her is as a welcoming hostess, Jesus and his disciples comfortable, at home, at meals, with Martha, Mary and Lazarus. But, she worries and frets, too busy, busy. But, we next see her in the Gospel of John, anxious about her brother Lazarus's illness, sending a message to Jesus, dismayed that he delayed and Lazarus had died, already four days in the tomb by the time that Jesus arrived. But, this is a moment of high signs and wonders, familiar from John's Gospel, Jesus miraculous, revealing his glory, an invitation to faith. Which Martha responds to perfectly, and is rewarded with the revelation that Jesus is the resurrection and the life. In the next chapter, rather quietly, friends and curious crowds from Jerusalem come to see

Lazarus. And there is Martha, back again, hosting the meal, back to her ordinary way of life, but faith-transformed.

So, here is a suggestion for the faith-journey of Thomas.

He is named in each of the synoptic gospels in the list of the chosen apostles. Interestingly, whether the list is hierarchical or not, he appears in eighth place! But, he is not singled out in the synoptic gospels at all. He follows his call. He listens to Jesus and, presumably, absorbs his teaching and spirit. He witnesses the miracles. He can ponder the parables. And, when Jesus sends out the 72, two by two, out he went, but Gospel-wise, anonymously.

In fact, his appearances, four of them, are in the gospel of John. And the reminder that John's Gospel was the last, compiled by the end of the first century, the stories told and retold over the decades. So, Thomas emerged somewhat in the life of the early church.

He is identified as Thomas, Didymus, the Twin (no further biographical detail). When we first hear him, the message has come from Martha and Mary for Jesus to heal their brother. With the pressure on Jesus, threats to him, and anticipation of his arrest, Thomas proclaims that they should all go with Jesus up to Bethany and, if necessary, die with him. (With the subsequent record of the apostles and the absence during Jesus' passion and death, this is on something of a par with the rash promises and declarations of Peter himself.)

There is no record of how he was affected by the raising of Lazarus from the dead. His next speaking part occurs during the Last Discourse. Jesus is reflecting, meditatively, on his mission, its accomplishment, his return to the Father. And the eager Thomas asks the question, "Lord, we do not know where you are going; how can we know the way to get there?", eliciting the immortal response from Jesus, 'I am the Way, the Truth', the Life, adding that no one goes to the Father except by me. Most don't remember that it was Thomas who asked the question but cherish and repeat Jesus answer. But, our thanks to Thomas for asking the question.

And, of course, the famous faith culmination in his journey. Why wasn't he in the upper room on the evening of the resurrection? Was he in the mode of the nickname given to him later, Doubting Thomas? But, when he is with the group in the upper room a week later, he has the touch of bombast. Certainly not ready to believe the eager eyewitness testimony of Mary Magdalene, Peter and John, the other apostles... Gregory the Great writes of Thomas' scepticism. This episode of doubt is certainly not a good character reference for Thomas. But, he is patiently one-upped by Jesus, having heard the rhetorical doubt, 'unless I see, unless I put my hand...' So, there is Jesus, taking up Thomas's challenge, inviting him, challenging him. But, as impulsively doubtful and doubting, Thomas is impulsively faith-fuelled, 'My Lord and My God'.

And, the lesson from Thomas' doubt and his faith-discovery the Gospel says is a message for all of us. Jesus chides him in a way by saying that he believed because of what he saw. Discipleship for ages to come is faith even though Jesus is not seen or heard as in the upper room.

Rather surprisingly, in the next and final chapter of the Gospel, some of the apostles are in Galilee with Peter, fishing. And, Thomas is in the list. Rehabilitated? Obviously after his experience, he had no desire to be on the outer.

So, thanks to Thomas, thanks to the Johannine community which may have been having its particular problems with members finding it hard to believe without seeing, for the stories of Thomas and faith.

(A postscript: Have you heard the story, which we heard in school back in the old days, that when Mary died, Thomas was absent again. When he arrived, he wanted to see Mary's body one more time. The other disciples took him to the tomb where Mary was laid – and she wasn't there! Thomas and the others had made a false assumption! An anecdote for celebrations on August 15th.)

Prepare Your Own Funeral Liturgy

No, this is not an intimation of a near or imminent death. Rather, it is an opportunity for scriptural reflection on one's life. One of the early chapters of *10 Minutes* was entitled Write Your Own Gospel. It was a suggestion to name and reflect on particular Gospel incidents, a miracle, an encounter with Jesus, a parable, a Nativity story, a Passion story, to help us appreciate our response to Jesus of the Gospels and his good news.

This particular exercise is directed towards this same appreciation and response. The invitation is to choose a Hebrew Scriptures' text, a New Testament text other than the Gospels and, of course, a Gospel text. Via the Scripture texts at the funeral liturgy, we are saying to those who mourn for us how we perceived our relationship with God to have been or, perhaps more accurately, what we had hoped a relationship with God had been. The chosen texts are a testimony to our faith, our hope, our love.

Because I had done a similar preparation for my Golden Jubilee of Ordination Mass, I decided that this would be the same for my funeral. However, I now have an opportunity to choose a Hebrew Scriptures text to add to the others from the Jubilee.

In fact, to set a tone, we sang the hymn of my MSC confrere, Frank Andersen, *Strong and Constant*, inspired by the saying of the Prophet, Jeremiah (31:3):

I have loved with an everlasting love, so I'm constant in my affection for you.

Frank's hymn is Strong and Constant.

I will be your God who walks with you.
You will be always within my hand.
Take your heart and give it all to me.
Strong and constant is my Love.
Strong and constant is my Love.

Should you wonder of far away from me,
I will search for you in every land.
Should you call then you will truly know
strong and constant is my Love.
Strong and constant is my Love

When you know sorrow within your life,
I will come, I will embrace your heart.
Through your pain you will discover me.
Strong and constant is my Love,
Strong and constant is my Love.

And, so to the first reading. I forget when I began to like the Canticle from the book of Daniel (3:3, 4, 6, 11-18). It recurs every four weeks in the prayer of the church, Morning Prayer, Week 4. It is a Canticle but it is a prayer characteristic of so much of the Hebrew Scriptures, a Lamentation. And, it is a Lamentation, not of an individual, but of the whole people. It is a rueful acknowledgement of the sad and imperfect world in which we live – and our own collective and personal contribution to that sad world because of our sinfulness. We acknowledge God is just in all that God has done for us – but we have lawlessly departed from God.

And it is a reminder that God's covenant is a pledge to love and mercy no matter what we do, no matter how far and how often we turn away. There is memory of the blessings given to the patriarchs but as acknowledgement that we are now bereft, brought low this day in all the world, searching for somewhere to settle and acknowledge our God. And then the shift to that Psalm-phrase, the acknowledgement of a contrite heart and a humble spirit, complete self-sacrifice on the part of the people and our individual selves, to be raised from shame, to trust in the covenant God, to follow and seek the face of God.

As we look back at our lives we can identify with the humbled people, the fearful situations in our lives. As I look back, I was born just before Hitler invaded Poland, the atomic bomb was dropped on Nagasaki on my sixth birthday, then the Iron Curtain descended, wars, especially for us in Vietnam, decades of Cold War and suspicions, surprising changes, the Berlin wall coming down, the official end of apartheid in South Africa, the independence of Timor-Leste ... But, 9/11, Afghanistan, Iraq, the Russian invasion of Ukraine. And, Covid 19. So much to lament. So much an incentive to trust and surrender.

Then a reading to remind us of what discipleship is, the pattern of Jesus, the ordinariness of our daily lives and challenge to deep personal commitment to others. In our minds (and hearts) we must be the same as Christ Jesus. That phrase comes at the end of the advice in Paul's letter to the Philippians, 2:1-5. I won't repeat the details here but if one is looking for a daily agenda of living in the spirit of Jesus, this passage, the second reading for the funeral liturgy, is a brief and wonderful summary.

And for the Gospel. All of us in our lives have had to exercise some kind of leadership, take on responsibilities, at home, in the community, in the workplace, our contribution to an orderly and safe world. My choice would be (I'm surprised because by temperament I would go to Luke's Gospel) the episode in Matthew (20) where the mother of James and John approaches Jesus demanding places at his side in the kingdom for her two sons – and the murmuring mutterings of jealousy of the other ten! Jesus' response is very clear. It is a pagan thing to lord it over others, "this is not to happen among you". If your ambition is to be great, then you must be the least, you must be a slave in your service of others just as Jesus came not to be served, but to serve. A meditation theme for anyone in a position of leadership, for anyone who exercises power.

And, perhaps during Communion, that most perfect Psalm, a most perfect poem in any language, 'The Lord is my Shepherd'. And/or, Andrew Lloyd Weber's *Requiem*.

I'm going to add the text of a hymn for moving from sanctuary to hearse. Our mother died when we were young, and so deprived of an experience of a mother's mothering, gratefully accepting the mothering of a grandmother in her late 60s and into her 70s, of a young aunt whose life was caring for her mother, taking us on in her late 20s. Over the years, through the influence of OLSH sisters and MSC confreres from school days on, I have learnt the place of Mary who gave Jesus his human heart. The hymn was written by James Maher MSC, untimely dying at age 52, a potential life of service cut short.

> In you our flesh he had to come
> You grounded him upon our earth
> Your feet that walked, your womb that held
> Your pain that brought this love to birth.
> The Sacred Heart of him you held
> Can grieve and grow within the space,
> Of patient love and listening;
> A mother's choice, a mystic's grace.
>
> In your delight, in your despair,
> The smallest choices of each day;
> The cost to you, your hope-filled yes,
> Your courage lived shows us the way.
> Our Lady of the Sacred Heart,
> Eternal sign of God surprise,
> In you we know the poor as blessed,
> This world transformed before our eyes.
>
> O Woman of the Sacred Heart,
> You heard the words of Gabriel.
> Pray we may hear the call of God

And come to meet Emmanuel
His truth is witnessed in your face,
That he became and was and is
The Sacred Heart, the resting place;
Our hearts forever held in his.

Rest in peace.

Appendix: Gospel Pointers to the Heart of Jesus

A good question: How do the Gospels reveal Jesus Heart? Some pointers.

Perhaps best to start with John's Gospel, chapter 1, opening up language of the Trinity, the beginning, the Word, the Word with God, is God. Then incarnation language, the Word made flesh, the Son, God's human experience, Jesus living our lives with us. But, this opening hymn of John's Gospel goes on to make quite clear who Jesus is, who the Son is, the Son who is nearest to the Father's heart – and, who in his life as the Word made flesh, has made known the very heart of God to us (John (14-18).

We know that Mark's Gospel is full of stories with great detail about what Jesus said and did. In terms of his heart, we can go to the end of chapter 1 (40-45), Jesus and the healing of the leper. Those who encountered Jesus seem to have responded so well to Jesus as a man of heart. The leper was prepared to disobey health regulations, no social distancing, eagerly came out of his quarantine. He was confident in the compassion of Jesus, 'if you want to, you can heal me'. The Jerusalem Bible translation emphasises Jesus' response, 'Of course, I want to...'. And, then, the literal outreach, personal touch and touching. The postscript of this story is that Jesus was prepared to forego the regulation in his compassion for the sick man. He accepted that for 40 days he would be leper. That meant sharing the leper's fate. He was relegated to quarantine outskirts. He was required to tear his clothes, muss his hair, throw dust on himself. He had to remain anonymous, keeping people away by calling out 'unclean'

Appendix: Gospel Pointers to the Heart of Jesus

We remember the tradition that Luke's Gospel was referred to as the Gospel of compassion. Any number of stories, any number of encounters, when Jesus revealed that he was a man of the heart. But, the heartiness of Jesus' extraordinary love is very clear in the stories he told, the parables which undercut assumptions about human care. In Luke 15, probably Jesus' most famous parable, referred to as the parable of The Prodigal Son, and, sometimes, The Prodigal Father, a suggestion I made in *10 Minutes* could be made that it could be called the parable of The Most Permissive Father. And, Jesus is telling us that this is what God, his father is like (and Jesus knows because he is nearest to the Father's heart). The father has no hesitation in giving into his son's unreasonable and presumptuous demand for his inheritance, allows him to go off, potentially to ruin his life. But he has never cut him off, the son can always return, not only repent, but experiences his father rushing to meet him, embracing, lavishing clothes and feast on him, rejoicing to recover his lost son. (And, calmly going out to reason with the unreasonable older son: 'everything I have is yours'.)

Which leaves the Gospel of Matthew. No surprise when we look at Chapter 11, Jesus' prayer of wonder to the father, revealing the love of God to those who might not have been expecting it. There are the words of his heart 'reassurance'. When we are tired, feeling overburdened, Jesus invites us to come to him and promises relief, assures us of respite and rest. And he can do this because he is gentle. He is in no way uppity, he is grounded, realistic about life, humble of – heart. But, after the rest, we are able to shoulder the yoke with Jesus, continue our life and work, but its demands seem lighter when carried with him.

We are blessed to have such solid grounding to develop our Spirituality of the Heart.

www.ingramcontent.com/pod-product-compliance
Lightning Source LLC
Chambersburg PA
CBHW012006090526
44590CB00026B/3902